WALLABY

by Annette
Annechild
and Russell
Bennett

# RECIPE FOR A GREAT AFFAIR

## *How to Cater Your Own Party . . . or Anybody Else's!*

*A WALLABY BOOK*
*Published by Simon & Schuster*
*New York*

Published by Wallaby Books
A Simon & Schuster Division of Gulf & Western Corporation
Simon & Schuster Building
1230 Avenue of the Americas
New York, New York 10020
WALLABY and colophon are registered trademarks of Simon & Schuster
Designed by Irving Perkins Associates
First Wallaby Books printing October 1981
Manufactured in the United States of America
Printed and bound by Maple-Vail Book Manufacturing Group
10  9  8  7  6  5  4  3  2  1

Annechild, Annette.
  Recipe for a great affair.
  1. Entertaining.  2. Cookery.  I. Bennett, Russell, 1949-  .  II. Title.
TX731.A65      642'.4      81-11606
                    AACR2

ISBN 0-671-42411-4

*Cover Credits:*
Stylist: Peggy Senatore
Flowers: Louis Homyac
Mr. Bennett's formal wear: Dunhill Tailors, New York
Food stylist: Russell Bennett
Jewelry: Black & Waslyn

To be able to entertain well in your own home is an ability that complements all facets of one's life. The popularity of home entertainment has increased steadily as the price of entertaining outside of the home has risen steadily. Catering businesses have sprung up all over the country in response to this blossoming trend.

Well, now *you* can take it one step further . . . you can cater your own party professionally yourself! You can save enormous amounts of money and have a lot of fun doing it as well. This book is a handbook of great affairs—a how-to book that enables you to cater everything from a smashing cocktail party to your daughter's wedding. By being able to do it yourself, you can save over 50 percent on the cost of every party that you have, and it's easy!

In fact, we've made it so simple that even if you hardly consider yourself a cook, you can serve thirty people a fabulous sit-down dinner or throw a sumptuous Sunday brunch with ease.

In this book it's all laid out, step by step: fabulous original easy-to-follow recipes, gourmet menu guides, and tips all along the way from top New York caterers. Even the grocery lists are made out for you—just tear them out on the perforated line and head for the grocery store!

So go ahead, have a lot of parties and a lot of fun . . . with:

*Recipe for a Great Affair!*

*this book is dedicated to*
*two winters—*
*a hard one in new york*
*and*
*a hot one in st. croix*

*with special thanks to*

Rick Bard . . . Joanna Lindquist . . . Vincent Nestico . . . Gene Brissie . . . Michael Desiato . . . John Latham . . . Bobby Goldberg . . . Joyce Golden . . . Ed and Eileen Friedman . . . Anne and Frank Viscardi . . . Steven Josephs . . . Vishnu Jayson . . . Laura . . . Granny . . . Renta Yenta . . . Jon Elliott . . . Aunt Jean and Uncle John . . . and to our invaluable assistant, Linda Chambers. . . . You are all an integral part of this book.

# The Natural Order of Things

# Welcome to Our Wonderful Affair

WHEN Russell Bennett and I first went into business, we felt we knew a lot about catering, but it was clear there was so much more to know. We began looking for reference material that would help us but found there was no book to refer to, no place to get the information up front that experience would someday provide. It simply did not exist, so we stopped looking and just began ourselves. . . . After years of working within every aspect of the food business, we finally came to learn the tricks, the shortcuts, the methods that would allow us to have even more fun and less hassle with each project we took on. As our confidence expanded and our successes grew, our interests in food stretched in new and different directions. I began writing in the food field, publishing *Getting into Your Wok with Annette Annechild* with Simon & Schuster, and Russell continued on to become a top New York caterer. His list of clients now includes Christian Dior, Broadway lighting designer Tharon Musser, New York's Ice Palace 57, A. M. Adler Fine Arts Galleries and Murjani Jeans; his guests have included Liza Minnelli, Gower Champion, Tennessee Williams, Jane Powell, Madeline Kahn, Arthur and Jeanne Ashe, and Maureen Stapleton, to name just a few.

Throughout the years, teaming up for special events and projects has been a favorite time for both of us. Finally, a book together seemed so natural, so right. We decided to collaborate on the book that we had searched the shelves for in our beginnings—a book about good foods at good parties, a book that kept in mind less-than-ideal kitchens, and far from extravagant budgets.

Here it is—our stories, our recipes, our notions about cooking, and our sense of fun doing what we love. Everything you need is on the next pages . . . with this book, you can cater everything from an office party to your daughter's wedding, a country picnic to a sophisticated cocktail party, all for many less dollars and with much more enjoyment than you would have ever thought possible. We hope the book serves you as well as our experiences have served us. Enjoy!

## Chapter 1

# How to Begin: Absolute Essentials in Your Kitchen

AS WITH MOST new projects, it only takes a bit of courage, or better yet, a sense of adventure to get started.

There are certain things that make a kitchen more fun to work in . . . most of these things are very basic and you probably have them already. We have listed in this first chapter everything you will need to produce all the parties in this book. The cost of new utensils, if any, is minimal.

If you are concerned about the size of your kitchen, rest easy: the kitchens that spawned both of the authors most people wouldn't have attempted making coffee in.

So, relax and have fun with it . . . you're about to throw some great parties and earn the reputation of a master chef!

AUTHORS' NOTE: There is, of course, no need to give these parties in any kind of order. However, the first party we've listed, "Cocktail Party for 20," is an ideal way to get started. It's followed by two different types of affairs—a buffet and a sit-down dinner. Once you've given these three parties you've covered the basics, which can then be applied to any size or type of affair.

## The Essentials

What you need, and a lot of what you probably have already:

### 1. KNIVES

A good sharp set is ideal; recommended is Ja Henckels, a combination of carbon and steel, which holds the edge better than any knife we've used. If you lack a full set, one can easily get by with one small utility knife, one butcher knife, one bread knife with a serrated edge, and most important, a sharpening steel or whetstone to keep your blades razor sharp, making your work easier as well as professional looking.

### 2. CUTTING BOARD

Wood or plastic will do. A good size would be approximately 10 inches by 15 inches. Your cutting board will also be used as a cheese board, so appearance should play an important part when selecting one.

## 3. BOWLS

Plastic bowls serve as good, all-purpose mixing bowls as well as storage containers, but are not recommended. Plastic is porous and tends to hold food odor and grease film. Best are stainless steel or ceramic, and the sizes to have on hand would be:

2 small 8 inch
3 medium 12 inch
2 large 20 inch
1 extra large tub, 2 to 4 gallons

These sizes are approximate and one usually has bowls in their kitchen to serve general cooking needs, but it will be important to have on hand the large tub for tossing or storing large amounts of food. A plastic dish pan will serve this purpose.

## 4. POTS AND PANS

"Pots and pans are my best friends in the kitchen. Some chefs swear by knives—others, various appliances. But I find I'm most dependent on my pots and pans. And, as with all my friends, I try to take care of them, and I'm careful on those I choose."—*Russell Bennett*

1   small 2-quart saucepan
2   large 8-quart saucepans
4–8 cookie sheets, medium-heavy metal
4   baking pans, 17 inches by 11½ inches x 2¼ inches
1   12 inches or larger skillet or wok
4   miniature muffin tins

## 5. UTENSILS

| | |
|---|---|
| wire whisk | set of measuring spoons |
| 2 wooden spoons | measuring cup (2-cup capacity) |
| ladle | large fork |
| rubber spatula | melon baller |
| slotted spoon | pastry blender |
| flipper | garlic press |
| heavy duty can opener | hand juicer |
| pepper grinder | grater |
| pastry bag (3 assorted tips) | potato peeler |
| colander | strainer |
| tongs | pastry brush |
| sifter | cooling racks |
| rolling pin | large serving spoon |
| meat thermometer | large Jell-O mold |
| oven timer | |

## 6. APPLIANCES

multispeed blender
electric mixer—either hand-held or stationary
food processor (optional)—a wonderful plus, but not necessary
*refrigerator space—calling on aid of friends and neighbors
* freezer space

## 7. PAPER AND PLASTIC PRODUCTS

gallon-size Ziploc bags
12-inch roll aluminum foil
18-inch roll aluminum foil
roll wax paper
several rolls paper towels
roll plastic wrap
freezer paper

trash bags, large and small
4 aluminum roasting pans
  (2 shallow, 2 deep)
plastic glasses
cocktail napkins
bamboo serving trays
baskets
ice

You won't find it necessary to keep in stock all of the above items unless you entertain frequently. Check the party plans for the affair, making sure your stock of supplies fulfill all the party needs.

## 8. EXTRAS

This would include items to help your kitchen run efficiently, although this list is probably the least important when it comes to essentials. Everyone has their own system of maintaining the kitchen, so these are a few suggestions of items that help us maintain ours.

pot holders (2, at least)
oven mitt
sponges
soap pads

oven cleaner
cotton or linen dish towels
  (4 to 6)
aprons (2)
grease-cutting detergent

* Both freezer and refrigerator space becomes crucial when entertaining large amounts of people. With careful planning, you can go a long way with what you have.

# Chapter 2

# First Time Out: Catering Your Own Cocktail Party for 20

THE FIRST TIME for anything is often the most difficult and always the most exciting. We have designed your first affair with that in mind. It is especially simple to create, and absolutely fun to be a part of. Just read through the entire chapter to get a general sense of it. Then follow the day-by-day, hour-by-hour instructions that will make your first affair truly unforgettable.

Amazingly enough, Russell's first cocktail party as a professional caterer was for Princess Ira von Furstenberg. After securing the job, Russell set to work on the perfect menu, which is in fact the very one that follows. Preparing for it, he checked and rechecked every detail. The time came, the food was loaded into the van and headed for the princess's New York hotel suite, 60 Park Avenue. He arrived only to find 60 Park Avenue was definitely not the princess's hotel. A panicked call to her office proved what he dreaded most: he had been given the wrong address. The actual address was 60th and Park, forty blocks away, and Russell and his crew were in New York rush hour traffic. As they inched through traffic with time clicking by, he began to realize the extent of the disastrous mix-up. The rental delivery company had also been given the wrong address, which meant no china, silver, or glassware, and perhaps the worst of it was, the liquor store delivery also would never arrive.

He arrived at the princess's suite long overdue to find the princess in rollers, screaming in Italian, with guests scheduled to arrive in half an hour. With admirable gumption, he still pulled the party off.

Russell called room service and ordered everything from china to liquor and immediately set up the food. By the time the guests arrived, the final touches were being placed on the food and out into the party it went. It was actually so successful, he was back two weeks later for the princess's next affair!

With much less trouble and a lot of fun, we hope you enjoy the recipes created for a princess.

## COCKTAIL PARTY FOR 20

# *Menu*

### COLD APPETIZERS

*Crudités with Avocado Dip\**
*Steak Tartare*
*Salmon Mousse Balls with Dill Sauce*

### HOT HORS D'OEUVRES

*Mushroom Caps Stuffed with Hot Sausage*
*Spinach Quiche Squares*

### DESSERT

*Chocolate-Covered Strawberries and Oranges*

*Full Bar Service*

\* An alternative to the Avocado Dip is the Caesar Dip on page
116, should avocados not be available or desired.

## *Bar Guide*
# The Standard Bar
(off brands unless indicated)

*Liquor:*   2 quarts vodka
2 quarts Scotch
1 bourbon

1 gin
2 magnums or 6 bottles Italian Soavé
1 pint dry vermouth

*Mixers:*   2 quarts orange juice
2 quarts club soda
2 quarts tonic
1 quart Coke

1 quart ginger ale
1 can tomato juice
3 limes
2 lemons

If a more prestigious bar is desired, and budget is not important, the following Bar Guide would be appropriate.

*Liquor:*   2 quarts Smirnoff
2 quarts Dewar's
1 quart Jack Daniel's
1 quart Beefeater

2 magnums Italian Soavé
1 pint Cinzano dry vermouth
1 pint Bacardi light rum
1 Harvey's Bristol Cream

*Mixers—*
*same as*
*standard*
*bar list*
*plus:*

1 lime juice
olives
onions
6 pack or 2 quarts mineral water

**Work Schedule**   We have created our party planning schedule for a party that would take place on a Saturday night at 5:00. If your party is in fact scheduled at a different time, simply adjust the work schedule appropriately. We have also broken down the full grocery list into separate lists for each day's preparation in the event that storage or freezer space would be limited.

# *Complete Grocery List*

**Produce:**
- 4 lemons
- 4 onions
- 1 bunch dill (or dried)
- 3 bunches fresh parsley (or dried)
- 1 head broccoli
- 1 head cauliflower
- 3 bunches scallions
- 2 pounds large mushrooms
- ½ pound string beans
- 2 large cucumbers
- 2 large summer squash
- 1 pint cherry tomatoes
- 1 bunch carrots
- 2 large zucchini
- 1 sweet red pepper
- 1 head red cabbage
- 2 large ripe avocados
- 1 garlic bulb
- 1 bunch watercress
- 2 boxes strawberries or
- 6 navel oranges or any combination of the two
- 1 head romaine

**Dry Goods:**
- 1 package gelatin
- 1 pound can red salmon
- 1 large jar mayonnaise
- Worcestershire sauce
- salt
- white pepper
- 2 boxes Melba Rounds
- paprika
- Dijon mustard
- celery salt
- lemon pepper
- marjoram
- sweet basil
- 1 2-ounce tube anchovy paste
- 1 4-ounce jar pimentos
- 5 pounds white flour, unbleached
- 1 can chicken broth
- 2 loaves party pumpernickel bread
- 1 can Italian seasoned breadcrumbs
- 1 can black olives (pitted)
- 1 small package chocolate chips
- 1 box semisweet Baker's chocolate
- oil
- paper towels
- 1 small jar capers

**Meat:**
- 2 pounds ground sirloin
- 1 pound hot Italian sausage

**Frozen:**
- 4 packages chopped spinach

**Dairy:**
- ½ pint heavy cream
- 1½ pints sour cream
- 2 pints half-and-half cream
- 2 dozen large eggs
- 1 pound butter
- 1½ pounds sharp Cheddar (whole)
- 1½ pounds Swiss (whole)
- 4 ounces grated Parmesan or Romano

*Liquor:* 1 bottle red wine for cooking
Bar Guide—see page 21

*Miscella-*
*neous:* plastic glasses (count 3 per person)
cocktail napkins (count 4 per
    person)
1 package doilies
flowers for garnish and centerpiece
5 serving trays—bamboo are
    especially nice

*Special* melon baller
*Equip-* blender
*ment:* 2 cookie sheets with raised edges
double boiler

## Party Plans

### Wednesday Evening or Thursday Afternoon

Food shop for quiche and mousse.

GROCERY LIST

4 lemons
3 onions
1 package gelatin
1 garlic bulb
2 bunches parsley or
   parsley flakes
1 pound can red salmon
1 large jar mayonnaise
½ pint heavy cream
½ pint sour cream
2 dozen large eggs
1½ pounds Swiss
   (whole)
1½ pounds sharp
   Cheddar (whole)
2 pints half-and-half
   cream

1 pound butter
Dijon mustard
2 boxes of Melba
   Rounds
5 pounds white flour,
   unbleached
1 can chicken broth
4 packages frozen
   chopped spinach
paprika
dill (dry)
white pepper
salt
lemon pepper (optional)
sweet basil
Worcestershire sauce

### Thursday Evening

Prepare Spinach Quiche Squares and Salmon Mousse Balls with Dill Sauce. See pages 34 and 32 for recipes.

### Friday

Everything but the meat (sirloin) can be shopped for on Friday. If you can pick up the bread on Saturday, you will be assured of the freshest possible.

GROCERY LIST

1 onion
2 pounds mushrooms
3 bunches scallions
1 bunch parsley
1 bunch watercress or
   2 parsley
2 large ripe avocados
1 head broccoli
1 head cauliflower
½ pound string beans
2 large cucumbers
2 large zucchini
2 large summer squash
1 sweet red pepper
1 pint cherry tomatoes
1 head red cabbage

1 head romaine
oil
1 can Italian seasoned
   breadcrumbs
marjoram
celery salt
1 pound hot Italian
   sausage
4 ounces grated
   Parmesan or Romano
   cheese
1 pint sour cream
1 bottle red wine (for
   cooking)
1 2-ounce tube anchovy
   paste

1 4-ounce jar pimentos
2 boxes strawberries or
6 oranges, or any
combination

1 package semisweet
chips
Baker's chocolate
1 small jar capers

See Bar Guide, page 21 and pick up liquor.

**Friday Evening**

Prepare Avocado Dip and Mushroom Caps. See pages 30 and 33 for recipes.
Set up bar.
Set up serving tables.

## Day of the Party

**Saturday**
9:00 A.M.

Pick up 2 pounds lean ground sirloin (fat and gristle removed), 2 party loaves pumpernickel bread, and flowers (2 bunches).

11:00 A.M. Prepare Crudités and arrange on tray, slicing all vegetables except romaine lettuce, which will be used for underlining on trays, and red cabbage, which will be cored and served as a crock for the dip and centered on tray.

NOON Prepare Steak Tartare.

1:00 P.M. Prepare Chocolate-Covered Strawberries and Oranges (see page 35)

2:00 P.M. Prepare trays:

a. Mushroom tray—underline and garnish one tray with romaine leaves and decorate with flowers. Leave mushrooms on cookie sheet to heat in oven.
b. Steak Tartare—garnish one tray and place Steak Tartare appetizers right on it, wrap and refrigerate.
c. Quiche—should be cut in 96 squares and left on cookie sheet. Have tray underlined with romaine and garnished with flowers and ready.
d. Dessert tray—should be garnished and ready, leave fruit on cookie sheet and store in refrigerator.
e. Salmon Mousse tray—follow directions for serving at end of recipe, page 32.

3:00 P.M. Check table. Put out ashtrays. *Get ice.* Relax!

4:00 P.M. Bathe, get dressed, and relax!

5:00 P.M. Greet guests and offer drinks. Preheat oven.

5:15 P.M.   Send out Crudités and Dip, Salmon Mousse tray and Steak Tartare. Heat mushrooms and quiche.

5:30 P.M.   Arrange two combinations of quiche and mushrooms on two remaining underlined hors d'oeuvre trays, send out; refill when necessary.

ENJOY!!

7:00 P.M.   Place fruit on waiting tray and serve this elegant final touch with pride.

CONGRATULATIONS!!

# Recipes

## Crudités with Avocado Dip

*Yield: 48 Squares*

### Crudités

INGREDIENTS:

1 bunch carrots
1 head broccoli
1 head cauliflower
1 bunch spring onions (scallions)
½ pound string beans
2 large cucumbers
2 large summer squash
2 large zucchini
1 sweet red pepper
1 medium-size head red cabbage
1 pint cherry tomatoes

1. Wash all vegetables thoroughly.
2. Cut into hors d'oeuvre-size pieces (see pages 195–197 for complete crudités instructions). Store in plastic bag.
3. Arrange on a tray when ready to serve. Bamboo slatted trays are now readily available at import shops. They are inexpensive and look beautiful lined with doilies and with the dip in a cored head of cabbage in the center.

### Avocado Dip

INGREDIENTS:

2 large ripe avocados
1 pint sour cream
¾ cup mayonnaise
1 teaspoon dill
1 clove garlic
1 bunch watercress
1 teaspoon Dijon mustard
½ teaspoon celery salt
½ teaspoon lemon pepper
1 teaspoon marjoram
   juice of 1 lemon
1 bunch scallions
   salt and pepper to taste
½ teaspoon sweet basil
2 tablespoons Worcestershire sauce

1. Combine all ingredients in blender.
2. Blend for about 30 seconds at high speed.
3. Place in a cored cabbage head and refrigerate covered.

## Steak Tartare

INGREDIENTS:

2 pounds lean sirloin, ground (fat and gristle removed)
1 large clove garlic
1 medium onion, cut up
½ bunch fresh parsley
3 tablespoons Worcestershire sauce
1 teaspoon Dijon mustard
1 tablespoon lemon juice
2 raw eggs
1 teaspoon lemon pepper
1 teaspoon anchovy paste
½ teaspoon celery salt
   salt and pepper to taste
2 tablespoons capers

1. Combine all ingredients except sirloin in blender for 30 seconds at high speed.
2. Add to ground meat and combine well.

### Garnish

INGREDIENTS:

2 hard-boiled eggs, chopped
1 small jar whole pimentos, slivered
2 small dark loaves of pumpernickel bread, sliced and quartered into 2-inch squares

1. Place meat on bread squares in small mounds.
2. Sprinkle with chopped egg.
3. Garnish with pimento slices.
4. Place on cookie sheets.
5. Cover securely with plastic wrap and store in refrigerator.

NOTE: Make sure this is the last appetizer to be prepared.

### Salmon Mousse Balls

## Salmon Mousse Balls with Dill Sauce

*Yield: Approximately 60 Melba Round Appetizers*

INGREDIENTS:

½ cup boiling water
2 tablespoons lemon juice
1 small onion, cut up
1 package gelatin
1 pound can red salmon
1 teaspoon paprika
1 teaspoon fresh or dried dill
½ cup mayonnaise
    dash Worcestershire sauce
½ teaspoon white pepper
½ teaspoon salt
1 cup heavy cream
2 boxes Melba Rounds

1. Blend first four ingredients at high speed for 20 seconds.
2. Add next seven ingredients, scraping edges. Blend again for 30 seconds at high speed.
3. With motor running at low speed, add heavy cream slowly.
4. Pour ingredients into bowl to gel (approximately 2 hours in refrigerator). It can also be frozen for later use.

### Dill Sauce

INGREDIENTS:

1 cup sour cream
¼ cup mayonnaise
1 tablespoon Dijon mustard
½ teaspoon dry or fresh dill
1 tablespoon lemon juice
    garnish with fresh dill

Mix all ingredients with wooden spoon till blended.

TO SERVE:

1. You will need a melon baller and 1 cup hot water. Dip baller in hot water and scoop out gelled salmon. Place 1 scoop on each Melba Round.
2. Top with Dill Sauce. Garnish with a sprig of fresh parsley.
3. Place on garnished tray and store in refrigerator.

## Mushroom Caps Stuffed with Hot Sausage

*Yield: Approximately 40 caps*

INGREDIENTS:

2 pounds large mushrooms (Clean, remove stems, and brush with cooking oil. Chop stems and set aside.)
oil for brushing caps
1 pound Italian sausages, out of skins
1 bunch scallions, minced fine
2 tablespoons butter
2 tablespoons fresh or dried parsley
1 cup Italian seasoned breadcrumbs
½ cup grated Parmesan or Romano cheese
¼–½ cup red wine
1 egg, beaten
pitted ripe black olives (sliced rounds)
romaine lettuce

1. Preheat oven to 375°.
2. Sauté sausage with scallions in butter till meat is no longer pink.
3. Add chopped mushroom stems, ¼ cup wine, bread crumbs, parsley and cheese. Sauté 5 minutes.
4. Remove from heat, let cool till lukewarm.
5. Blend in 1 beaten egg with hands.
6. If mixture seems too dry for stuffing add rest of wine.
7. Stuff oiled caps and garnish with sliced black olives. Place on cookie sheet, cover tightly and refrigerate.
8. Just before serving bake for 10–12 minutes.
9. Garnish with sliced black olives and romaine lettuce leaves.

## Spinach Quiche Squares

*Yield: 96 Squares†*

### Dough*

INGREDIENTS:

2 cups white flour, unbleached
½ cup butter
½ teaspoon salt
5 tablespoons ice water

### Filling

INGREDIENTS:

2 packages frozen chopped spinach, defrosted and press dried
1½ pounds shredded cheese (¾ sharp Cheddar, ¾ Swiss)
7 large grade A eggs
2 cups half-and-half
1 small onion
½ can chicken broth
½ teaspoon salt
1 teaspoon lemon pepper (optional)
1 tablespoon Worcestershire sauce
1 teaspoon sweet basil
3 tablespoons parsley (flakes or fresh)
1 large clove garlic

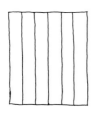

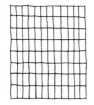

1. Blend first three ingredients till texture is crumbly. You can use a pastry blender or the knife and fork method.
2. Add water 1 tablespoon at a time till dough pulls together.
3. Form into ball and refrigerate 30 minutes.
4. Preheat oven to 375° and prepare filling by blending ingredients for 30 seconds at high speed.
5. Roll dough into a rectangle larger than your cookie sheet, then place dough on sheet.
6. Crimp edges ¼-inch higher on sides than the sheet to form rim.
7. Lay cheese on bottom of shell.
8. Add filling.
9. Lay spinach on top and pat lightly.
10. Bake for 45 minutes or until golden brown.
11. Store in refrigerator or freezer on cookie sheet.
12. Cut into 96 squares before serving.

\* For the dough, you will need a cookie sheet with raised edges all around.
† To get 96 squares out of one sheet of quiche, cut in half lengthwise, then cut each half in half lengthwise, then cut each quarter in half lengthwise, then turn and repeat widthwise.

## *Chocolate-Covered Strawberries and Oranges*

*Yield: Approximately 35 pieces*

INGREDIENTS:

2 boxes fresh whole strawberries or 6 navel oranges in sections, or any combination of the two
1 small package semisweet chocolate chips
2 squares semisweet Baker's chocolate
1 tablespoon oil

1. Heat chocolate chips and squares with oil over low flame in double boiler.
2. Dip cleaned and dried fruit into chocolate.
3. Place on greased cookie sheet.
4. Refrigerate until chocolate has hardened.

## Chapter 3

# Come Celebrate: A Beautiful Buffet for 50

AH! NOW THAT you have experienced the splash of your gala cocktail party, it's time to embark on the festive occasion of a Beautiful Buffet for 50.

The menu is a smashing surprise—crepes! Yes, crepes for fifty, after delectable Zucchini Cups Stuffed with Crabmeat and Tomato Quiche Squares for appetizers. The main course is accompanied by a fresh Apple Relish and a Caesar Salad. The grand finale of this affair is luscious Oranges Grand Marnier.

After reading through the chapter, enjoy the step-by-step instructions that will make you a master of crepes and quite the accomplished caterer!

## BEAUTIFUL BUFFET FOR 50

# Menu

**APPETIZERS**

*Zucchini Cups Stuffed with Crabmeat*
*Miniature Tomato Quiche Squares*

**ENTRÉES**

*Chicken and Mushroom Crepes*
*Spinach Walnut Crepes*
*with Sauce Mornay*

**RELISH**

*Tangy Apple Relish*

**SALAD**

*Caesar Salad*

**DESSERT**

*Oranges Grand Marnier*

*Beer and Wine Service*

# Buffet Bar*

2 cases white wine
4 cases beer (domestic)
6 quarts Coke
2 quarts Tab
2 quarts ginger ale
2 quarts 7-Up
2 quarts orange juice

If a more prestigious bar is desired:

*Liquor:*   3 quarts vodka
3 quarts Scotch
2 quarts bourbon
1 quart gin
1 pint dry vermouth
2 cases white wine

*Mixers:*   6 quarts mineral water
3 quarts orange juice
4 quarts club soda
3 quarts tonic
2 quarts Coke
2 quarts Tab
3 quarts ginger ale
38 ounces tomato juice
6 limes
3 lemons

* Eight pounds of ice serves forty people per hour.

# Complete Grocery List

**Produce:**
- 20 5-inch zucchini
- 1 dozen lemons
- 4 bunches parsley
- 1 bunch dill (fresh or dried)
- 1 garlic bulb
- 1 onion
- 3 pounds fresh or canned mushrooms
- ½ pound shallots
- 6 bunches scallions
- 3 pounds walnut pieces
- 25 red Delicious apples
- 10 heads romaine lettuce
- 35–40 navel oranges
- 8 ounces slivered almonds

**Dry Goods:**
- 1 medium jar mayonnaise
- Dijon mustard
- Worchestershire sauce
- 10 pounds white flour, unbleached
- 9 13-ounce cans chicken broth*
- 2 large cans peeled whole tomatoes
- 1 quart peanut oil
- 1 small bottle olive oil
- 1 large box Italian seasoned breadcrumbs
- 1 4-ounce tube anchovy paste
- 2 boxes seasoned croutons
- cinnamon
- sesame seeds
- white pepper
- 1 8-ounce jar honey
- tarragon
- basil
- lemon pepper
- celery salt
- salt and pepper
- rice or wine vinegar
- 1 8-ounce package shredded coconut

**Dairy:**
- 1 quart and ½ pint sour cream
- 3 dozen eggs
- 2 pints half-and-half cream
- 1½ pounds Swiss cheese
- 1½ pounds Cheddar cheese
- 2 pounds Parmesan cheese
- 1 gallon plus 1 quart milk
- 1 quart heavy cream
- 2 pounds butter

**Poultry and Fish:**
- 5 pounds fresh or frozen crabmeat
- 16 pounds boneless, skinless breast of chicken (Ask butcher to save bones)

* If using homemade chicken broth in Sauce Mornay you would only need 5 cans broth. If using water instead of broth in crepe batter recipe you would need only 7 cans.

| | |
|---|---|
| ***Paper and Plastic Products:*** | 75 10-inch sturdy paper plates<br>100 dinner-size napkins<br>75 dessert bowls<br>75 each plastic forks and dessert spoons |
| ***Frozen:*** | 20 packages frozen chopped spinach |

| ***Special Equipment:*** | | |
|---|---|---|
| oblong chafing dish (2 gallons, 2 compartments) | | salad bowl |
| 1 punch bowl | | flowers (optional) |
| 2 galvanized ice tubs | | 2 crepe pans |
| silverware and serving utensils | | grater |
| 2 platters | | melon baller |
| 1 tray | | blender |
| | | 2 cookie sheets with raised edges |

| | |
|---|---|
| ***Liquor:*** | 1 bottle white wine<br>½ pint dry vermouth<br>1 pint Triple Sec<br>1 pint Grand Marnier<br>Buffet Bar (see page 41) |

## Party Plans

We have developed a party plan for a party scheduled on Saturday at 8:00 P.M. The plan can be adjusted easily according to your needs. We have broken the total grocery list down day by day to assure the freshest food and to help those with limited storage and freezer space.

### Saturday

Grocery shop for Miniature Tomato Quiche Squares, crepe batter, and liquor. Bar definitely should be stocked on this Saturday.

GROCERY LIST

| | |
|---|---|
| milk | 1½ pounds Cheddar cheese |
| 1–3 cans chicken broth | basil |
| 4 ounces Parmesan cheese | parsley |
| 10 pounds flour | 2 pints half-and-half cream |
| 2 pounds butter | 2 small onions |
| ½ gallon milk | lemon pepper |
| oil | 2 large cans whole tomatoes |
| 3 dozen eggs | Worcestershire sauce |
| 1½ pounds Swiss cheese | salt and pepper |

Assuming you have more time and possibly a little help on Saturday, you might want to pick up all other dry goods and frozen foods and liquor for cooking and bar.

### Sunday and Monday evenings

Prepare crepes. See page 50 for recipe.

### Tuesday afternoon

Call and order chicken and shop for Wednesday.

### Tuesday evening

Prepare quiches. See page 49 for recipe.

### Wednesday evening

Prepare both fillings. See pages 50–51 for recipes.

GROCERY LIST

| | |
|---|---|
| 16 pounds boneless, skinless chicken breasts | tarragon |
| | sesame seeds |
| 3 pounds fresh or canned mushrooms | 20 packages frozen spinach |
| | 6 bunches scallions |
| ½ pound shallots | 3 cans chicken broth |
| 1 quart heavy cream | seasoned breadcrumbs |
| 1 bottle white wine | 3 pounds walnuts |
| 1 pint vermouth | basil |
| 1 bunch parsley | 1 quart sour cream |

### Thursday

Sauce Mornay and dressing for salad. See page 52 for recipes.

See page 52 for recipes.

GROCERY LIST

4 cans or homemade
  chicken stock
4 quarts milk
2 pounds grated Parmesan
  cheese
white pepper
bottled or fresh lemon
  juice
1 4-ounce tube anchovy
  paste

rice or wine vinegar
Worcestershire sauce
garlic
olive oil
1 quart peanut oil
seasoned croutons and
  romaine lettuce can be
  picked up now or later

### Friday

Prepare Zucchini Cups, see page 48 for recipe, set up bar.

see page 48 for recipe

GROCERY LIST

20 5-inch zucchini
5 pounds fresh or frozen
  crabmeat
mayonnaise
sour cream

fresh or dried parsley
dill
Dijon mustard
celery salt
juice of 2 lemons

## Day of the Party

### Saturday

9:00 A.M.  Last minute shopping.

GROCERY LIST

10 heads romaine lettuce
35–40 navel oranges
shredded coconut
slivered almonds
25 red Delicious apples

8 ounces honey
cinnamon
flowers for garnish and
  centerpiece (optional)

11:00 A.M.  Prepare Oranges Grand Marnier. See page 53 for recipe.

NOON  Prepare Tangy Apple Relish. See page 52 for recipe.

1:00 P.M.  Set up tables for serving and have lunch.

2:00 P.M.  Clean salad, dry well, tear into bite-size pieces.

3:00 P.M.  Arrange centerpiece and place on table.

4:00 P.M.  Garnish tray for Zucchini Cups, arrange Zucchini Cups on it, and refrigerate.

See page 53 for recipe. See page 52 for recipe.

| | |
|---|---|
| 4:30–6:00 P.M. | Bathe, relax, enjoy! |
| 6:00 P.M. | Take crepes out of freezer to defrost. |
| 7:00 P.M. | Garnish trays for quiche, have them ready to be filled and served. |
| 7:30 P.M. | Preheat oven to 350°. |
| Approximately 8:00 P.M. (or when all your guests have arrived) | a. Place quiche in oven for 15 minutes.<br>b. Place crepes, still wrapped in aluminum foil, in oven with quiche for 15 minutes.<br>c. Warm the two fillings in separate saucepans on top of the stove over low heat. |
| 8:10 P.M. | Toss salad, top with croutons and cheese. If you don't have a bowl large enough for tossing the salad, it can be tossed in a plastic garbage bag. Don't be afraid to use your hands! Place in serving bowl and place on table. |
| 8:15 P.M. | Put cold appetizers on serving table. |
| 8:20 P.M. | a) Take quiche from oven, place on garnished trays, put on serving table.<br>b) Take crepes from oven, place in stacks on serving platter, put on serving table.<br>c) Take filling from heat, place in serving bowls, put on serving table. |
| 8:30 P.M. | a. Dinner is served. We suggest that you let people roll their own crepes at the buffet table. However, we have found that it is important to demonstrate the first one and thereafter to serve the fillings onto the crepes for the guests. Remember, your fillings are portioned out for 50 people, so ladle about ½ cup onto each crepe.<br>b. When everyone has been served, clear buffet table, and set up for dessert.<br>c. Serve oranges from bowl in center of table.<br>d. Now relax, and most of all, enjoy your great party!!! |

# Recipes

## Zucchini Cups Stuffed with Crabmeat

*Yield: Approximately 100 cups*

INGREDIENTS:

20 5-inch zucchini
5 pounds fresh or frozen crabmeat
    juice of 2 lemons
¼ cup mayonnaise
¼ cup sour cream
3 tablespoons dried or fresh parsley
1 tablespoon dried or fresh dill
    fresh ground pepper and salt to taste
1 teaspoon Dijon mustard
1 clove garlic
1 tablespoon Worcestershire sauce
1 teaspoon celery salt

1. Scrub zucchini and trim off ends.
2. Cut into 1-inch long pieces.
3. Scoop out inside with small melon baller, taking care not to pierce bottom.
4. Combine all ingredients but crabmeat and zucchini in blender.
5. Blend at high speed for 30 seconds.
6. Mix blended ingredients with crabmeat.
7. Stuff zucchini cups with crabmeat.
8. Put on cookie sheet and refrigerate.

## Miniature Tomato Quiche Squares

*Yield: 96 squares per cookie sheet**

(You will have to make the entire quiche recipe twice.)

### Dough

INGREDIENTS:

2 cups white flour, unbleached
½ cup butter
½ teaspoon salt
5 tablespoons ice water

### Filling

(This recipe will fill your blender jar twice so divide ingredients into two batches.)

INGREDIENTS:

1 large can whole tomatoes, drained and squeezed out
1½ pounds shredded cheese (¾ each of Swiss and Cheddar)
¼ cup Parmesan Cheese
8 eggs
2 cups half-and-half cream
1 small onion
½ can chicken broth
½ teaspoon salt
1 teaspoon lemon pepper
1 tablespoon Worcestershire sauce
1 teaspoon basil
4 tablespoons parsley

1. Blend first three ingredients with pastry cutter till texture is crumbly.
2. Add water 1 tablespoon at a time till dough pulls together.
3. Form into ball and refrigerate ½ hour.
4. Preheat oven to 375° and prepare filling by blending all ingredients 30 seconds at high speed.
5. Then roll out dough into a rectangle larger than cookie sheet.
6. Crimp edges up to form rim ¼-inch high.
7. Lay Cheddar and Swiss shredded cheese on bottom of shell.
8. Add filling.
9. Top with tomatoes, pressing tomatoes through your fingers to spread evenly.
10. Sprinkle with ¼ cup Parmesan cheese.
11. Bake for 45 minutes or till golden brown.

* See page 34 for cutting instructions.

## Crepes for 50

*Yield: 150 crepes*

Great for making ahead. We suggest making the batter half at a time and planning one long, or two short evenings' work. You'll need two crepe pans.

INGREDIENTS:

9 tablespoons butter
9 eggs
4 cups milk
3 cups water (or chicken stock, optional)
1½ teaspoons salt
6 cups flour
oil to grease crepe pans

1. Melt butter in saucepan over low heat.
2. Whisk eggs till lightly beaten in largest available bowl.
3. Add milk, water, and salt and whisk together.
4. Gradually add in flour with whisk.
5. Blend in butter. It should be the consistency of heavy cream —add more water if necessary.
6. Refrigerate 2 hours or overnight.

TO PREPARE CREPES:

1. Heat pans over medium high heat.
2. Grease pans lightly.
3. Ladle on approximately 3 tablespoons batter.
4. Swirl till pan is coated. Pour off extra batter into bowl.
5. Fry till underside is golden brown.
6. Flip with fingers or spatula.
7. Cook other side 30 seconds.
8. Flip off into paper towels to cool.
9. Stack in groups of 20, wrap in tin foil, and freeze.

### Crepe Fillings
*Chicken and Mushrooms*
   *Yield: 75 crepes*

Again you can make the recipe all at once in a very large pot or make half at a time, more conveniently.

INGREDIENTS:

16 pounds of boned, skinned chicken breasts
3 pounds mushrooms
½ pound shallots
½ cup butter
3 tablespoons sesame seeds
4 cups heavy cream
1 cup chopped fresh or dried parsley

2 tablespoons tarragon
    salt and pepper to taste
1 cup white wine
1 cup flour

1. Cut chicken into small strips.
2. Wash mushrooms and slice thinly.
3. Peel and mince shallots.
4. Melt butter in large pot.
5. Sauté shallots for 2 to 3 minutes.
6. Add chicken strips; sauté till they begin to turn white.
7. Add sesame seeds and mushrooms. Cook till soft.
8. Add cream, parsley, tarragon, salt, and pepper.
9. Cook 5 minutes.
10. In a small bowl gradually add flour to wine with wire whisk and add to chicken.
11. Cook 10 to 15 minutes till consistency of a thick stew; refrigerate.

*Spinach Walnut*
    *Yield: 75 crepes*

INGREDIENTS:

20 packages frozen chopped spinach, defrosted
 6 bunches spring onions (scallions)
 ½ cup butter
2–3 cans chicken broth
 1 cup vermouth
 3 pounds coarsely chopped walnuts
 4 tablespoons basil
 1 quart sour cream
    salt and pepper to taste
 3 cups seasoned breadcrumbs

1. Drain and press water from spinach.
2. Chop spring onions.
3. Sauté onions with ½ cup butter in large pot.
4. Add spinach and sauté 3 minutes.
5. Add 2 cans broth, vermouth, walnuts, basil, sour cream, salt, and pepper. Stir.
6. Add breadcrumbs. Stir again.
7. If consistency is very thick, add more broth.
8. Simmer 10 minutes.
9. Store in refrigerator.

## Sauce Mornay for Crepes

*Yield: 24 cups*

INGREDIENTS:

8 cups chicken stock (homemade or canned stock)
1 cup flour
4 quarts milk
1 pound grated Parmesan cheese
   salt to taste
1 tablespoon white pepper

1. Melt butter in an 8-quart pan.
2. Whisk in flour.
3. Add stock while whisking.
4. Add milk, Parmesan cheese, salt, and pepper, and continue whisking.
5. Cook till creamy.
6. Refrigerate.

## Tangy Apple Relish

INGREDIENTS:

25 red Delicious apples, cored but not peeled, shredded*
1 cup lemon juice
1 cup honey
   cinnamon

1. Toss all ingredients together.
2. Top with a sprinkle of cinnamon.

   * As you are grating apples, sprinkle with a bit of the lemon juice to avoid browning.

## Caesar Salad for 50

INGREDIENTS:

10 heads romaine lettuce
2 cups Parmesan cheese
½ cup lemon juice
2 eggs, raw
½ tube (2 ounces) anchovy paste
½ cup rice or wine vinegar
3 cloves garlic
4 tablespoons Worcestershire sauce
1 quart peanut oil
½ cup olive oil
1 package seasoned croutons (homemade is better)

1. Wash lettuce and tear into bite size pieces. Pat or spin dry.
2. To make dressing, blend all ingredients together except croutons, lettuce, and 1 cup Parmesan. Store.
3. Refrigerate.
4. When ready to serve, toss lettuce with dressing and top with remaining Parmesan cheese and croutons.

## Oranges Grand Marnier for 50

**INGREDIENTS:**

35–40 navel oranges
1 cup Triple Sec
1 cup Grand Marnier
1 cup shredded coconut
1 cup slivered almonds

1. Grate enough orange peels to yield 2 cups.
2. Peel and slice oranges across to form round slices.
3. In a large bowl put slices, Triple Sec, peels, and Grand Marnier.
4. Marinate overnight in refrigerator.
5. Top with coconut and slivered almonds before serving.

Chapter 4

# Sit Down and Enjoy: Dinner for 30

ONCE YOU HAVE experienced the success of your first cocktail party and your Beautiful Buffet for 50 and have basked in the warm glow of praise and personal pride . . . you will be in the perfect frame of mind for this chapter. This one takes you through the grand accomplishment of serving thirty people an elegant sit down dinner.

The menu begins with a delicious Shrimp Mousse topped with Sauce Verte, proceeds to an awesome Roast Veal Demiglace, stuffed with spinach and pecans, and is accompanied by Herbed Rice, Zucchini Rapé, and a Boston Lettuce-Sesame Salad. All of this is gloriously topped off with home-baked Kahlua Hazelnut Torte. This menu was originally created for A. M. Adler Fine Art Galleries. It debuted at a private collection exhibition of the United States premiere of the renowned French artist, Jules Pascin.

This party will take more preparation than the first two, but it is equally easy. The steps are carefully laid out for you, the grocery lists made. Once again, read through the entire chapter first; also read about rentals and staffing in chapter 14, then go back to the beginning and follow the simple steps to a spectacular do-it-yourself, gourmet evening!

*SIT DOWN DINNER FOR 30*

# *Menu*

**APPETIZER**

*Shrimp Mousse with Sauce Verte*

**ENTRÉE**

*Roast Veal Demiglace with Spinach Pecan Stuffing
Served with Herbed Rice*

**VEGETABLE**

*Zucchini Rapé*

**SALAD**

*Boston Lettuce with Mushrooms and Sesame Seeds
with Creamy Italian Dressing*

**DESSERT**

*Kahlua Hazelnut Torte*

*Dry White and Bordeaux Wine*

# Complete Grocery List

**Produce:**
6 lemons
1 pound small yellow onions
3 bunches parsley (fresh or dried)
1 garlic bulb
1 bunch dill (fresh or dried)
15 large zucchini
1 bunch celery

3 large carrots
8 heads Boston lettuce
3 pounds fresh mushrooms
1 box cherry tomatoes
3 bunches watercress
2 large potatoes
½ pound shallots

**Dry Goods:**
1 pound hazelnut pieces
5 pounds sugar
1 small jar instant espresso
vanilla extract
1 box unflavored gelatin
3 cans chicken broth
1 large jar mayonnaise
1 can unflavored breadcrumbs
kosher salt
white pepper
celery salt
1 tube anchovy paste
1 pound coffee
rice or wine vinegar
1 jar Dijon mustard
2 quarts peanut oil
Worcestershire sauce

1 3-pound box long grain rice
1 small jar honey
whole cloves
1 small package seasoned
   breadcrumbs
sage
1 pound white flour, unbleached
baking powder
bay leaves
½ pound pecan pieces
½ pound sesame seeds
salt and pepper
oregano
basil
tarragon
dill

**Meat and Fish:**
1½ pounds fresh shrimp (or frozen)
2 7-pound boned shoulders of veal
veal bones

**Frozen:**
4 packages frozen chopped spinach

**Dairy:**
2 dozen eggs
1 stick sweet butter
1 quart heavy cream
1 pint buttermilk

1 pound butter
1 quart milk
2 pints half-and-half cream

| | |
|---|---|
| *Liquor:* | 9 bottles dry white wine |
| | 1 pint Kahlua |
| | 1 case Bordeaux red wine |
| *Special Equip-ment:* | ball of twine |
| | blender |
| | grater |

## Party Plans

### Monday

Shop for Kahlua Hazelnut Torte, Demiglace, Creamy Italian Dressing, Shrimp Mousse, and Sauce Verte ingredients. It would also be good, at this time, to order and pick up your liquor supply.

GROCERY LIST

baking powder
2 dozen eggs
1 pound hazelnut pieces
5-pound bag sugar
1 small jar instant espresso
vanilla extract
6 lemons
1 box unflavored gelatin
1 can chicken broth
1½ pounds fresh or frozen shrimp
1 large jar mayonnaise
1 pound small yellow onions
3 bunches parsley (fresh or dried)

1 can unseasoned breadcrumbs
1 quart heavy cream
salt
white pepper
celery salt
1 tube anchovy paste
rice or wine vinegar
garlic bulb
Dijon mustard
dill (dried or fresh)
1 small bottle of olive oil
2 quarts peanut oil
Worcestershire sauce
1 pint buttermilk
oregano

LIQUOR LIST

9 bottles dry white wine (1 for cooking, 8 to serve with appetizer)

1 pint Kahlua
1 case Bordeaux red wine (to serve with dinner)

### Tuesday

a. Your party help should, at this time, be arranged for. If it hasn't been, do it now.
b. Phone in the rental order during business day.
c. Prepare two recipes of Kahlua Hazelnut Torte (see recipe, page 68) and freeze.
d. Confirm the number of your dinner guests for Saturday.
e. Prepare Creamy Italian Dressing. See recipe, page 67.

### Wednesday

Prepare Shrimp Mousse (see recipe, page 63), cover tightly, and refrigerate.

### Thursday

Shop for all other ingredients, prepare Demiglace (recipe is on page 64), and, if you have enough energy left after all that shopping, you could prepare the Sauce Verte (see page 64), for the Shrimp Mousse, otherwise do it at your convenience.

1 3-pound box long grain
    rice
2 cans chicken broth
1 pound butter
15 large-size zucchini
½ pound shallots
1 bunch celery
3 large carrots
8 heads Boston lettuce
    (store in plastic bags, if
    space is a problem, pick
    up Saturday)
2 large potatoes
3 pounds fresh
    mushrooms
1 quart milk
1 small jar honey
ball of twine
whole cloves
1 small package seasoned
    breadcrumbs

sage
tarragon
1 pound white flour,
    unbleached
bay leaves
½ pound pecan pieces
½ pound sesame seeds
kosher salt
4 packages frozen chopped
    spinach
2 7-pound boned
    shoulders of veal (ask
    butcher for bones, and
    ask to cut bones to size
    to fit stockpot)
1 pound coffee
2 pints half-and-half cream
1 box cherry tomatoes*
3 bunches watercress*

**Friday**

a. Prepare Spinach Walnut Stuffing for veal and store in container tightly covered.
b. Continue checking the Demiglace.
c. Shred the zucchini, squeezing out the water, and store in an airtight container.
d. If Sauce Verte has not been prepared, you can do it now.

*Day of the Party*  **Saturday**

9:00 A.M.  a. After coffee, continue simmering Demiglace if necessary.
           b. Prepare Roast Veal, stuff, and tie back in place. Place roast in preheated 350° oven and begin baking for 2½ hours.

10:30 A.M.  Clean the lettuce and dry well. Wash and slice the mushrooms. Toss together with sesame seeds and refrigerate in plastic bag.

11:30 A.M.  Finish preparing Demiglace by completing the last step in the recipe instructions.

NOON  a. Remove veal from oven, let cool, and refrigerate.
        b. Enjoy a quiet lunch.

* Two bunches watercress, plus box of cherry tomatoes for garnish. Wrap tightly and refrigerate.

| 1:00 P.M. | a. Prepare rice, let cool, put in a baking pan, set aside. |
|---|---|
| | b. While rice is cooking, unmold mousse, cover and refrigerate. |
| 2:00 P.M. | Arrange flowers on tables and make seating arrangement chart. See chapter 14, "Planning Large Affairs." |
| 3:00 P.M. | Tidy up kitchen. |
| 4:00 P.M. | Bathe, relax. |
| 6:00 P.M. | Staff arrives, follow chapter 14. |
| 8:00 P.M. | Sit down. Enjoy. |

## Shrimp Mousse

(Make two batches, one at a time.)

INGREDIENTS:

1 tablespoon lemon juice
2 envelopes gelatin
1 small onion quartered
⅓ cup white wine
⅓ cup chicken stock or broth
3 separated eggs
1 cup cooked coarsely cut up shrimp*
½ cup mayonnaise
1 tablespoon parsley
1 cup heavy cream
½ teaspoon salt
½ teaspoon white pepper
½ teaspoon celery salt
1 tablespoon anchovy paste

1. Place lemon juice, gelatin, and onion into blender; heat in saucepan wine and stock, then add and blend at high speed for 20 seconds.
2. Add remaining ingredients except egg whites and cream. Blend at high speed 15 seconds while slowly pouring in heavy cream through cover hole.
3. In large stainless steel bowl, beat egg whites till stiff. Fold blender ingredients into whites.
4. Pour into 4-cup mold; chill until set.
5. Unmold and serve.

* From the 1½ pounds of shrimp purchased for both batches, hold out 15 nicely shaped shrimp, slice in half lengthwise, for garnish after cooking. To store, place in cold water, cover tightly, keep in refrigerator.

## Sauce Verte

INGREDIENTS:

2 eggs
4 tablespoons lemon juice
2 tablespoons rice or wine vinegar
½ teaspoon salt
½ teaspoon white pepper
1 tablespoon Worcestershire sauce
1 tablespoon fresh or dried dill
⅓ cup olive oil
1 clove garlic
2 tablespoons Dijon mustard
3 cups peanut oil
1 bunch watercress

1. Blend all ingredients except peanut oil and watercress at high speed for 10 seconds.
2. Pour peanut oil slowly through hole in cover with motor running. Sauce will thicken.
3. Add watercress and blend till sauce is green with small flecks of watercress.
4. Refrigerate.

## Roast Veal Stuffed with Spinach and Pecans with Demiglace

INGREDIENTS:

2 7-pound wrapped boned shoulder veals (ask butcher for veal bones for Demiglace, which must be prepared 2 days ahead)
twine

### Demiglace

INGREDIENTS:

1 large onion studded with cloves
4 stalks celery
2 carrots, cut into large pieces
2 cloves garlic
veal bones
salt to taste
2 tablespoons butter
2 tablespoons flour

1. Put all ingredients in an 8-quart pot.
2. Cover with water till ¾ full.
3. Simmer 24 hours, strain. The water level should be checked every couple of hours; the final product will boil down to approximately 2 quarts.
4. Strain and refrigerate.
5. Salt to taste.

6. Over low heat, combine 2 tablespoons butter with 2 table-spoons flour, stir constantly for 3 minutes and then add to Demiglace.
7. This should be put in a container and set aside.

### Spinach Pecan Stuffing and Veal Preparation

INGREDIENTS:

    4 packages frozen chopped spinach, defrosted
    ½ cup breadcrumbs
    ¼ cup sweet vermouth
       pinch of sage
    2 teaspoons basil
       salt and pepper to taste
    1 cup chopped pecans
    ½ stick sweet butter
    1 carrot, cut into large pieces
    2 large potatoes, cut into chunks

1. Preheat oven to 325°.
2. Mix all ingredients, except carrots and potatoes, in bowl.
3. Prepare veal by slitting in shape of a Y ¾ way through veal.
4. Stuff with filling.
5. Tie back with twine.
6. Place both veal shoulders in large roasting pan with potatoes, carrots (the vegetables will prevent the veal from drying out).
7. Roast for 3½ hours (veal is roasted for approximately 30 minutes per pound).

**Herbed Rice**

INGREDIENTS:

6 cups long grain white rice
2 cans chicken stock (broth)
8½ cups water
1 tablespoon Worcestershire sauce
2 garlic cloves
½ cup chopped parsley
1 tablespoon basil
½ teaspoon tarragon
2 bay leaves
1 teaspoon dill
3 tablespoons butter
salt and pepper to taste

1. Add all ingredients to a large saucepan; bring to a boil.
2. Reduce heat and simmer for 17 minutes.
3. Remove from heat and transfer to a baking pan and let cool; cover with foil.

**Zucchini Rapé**

INGREDIENTS:

15 large zucchini
kosher salt
½ pound shallots or scallions
2 cloves garlic
½ cup vegetable oil
1 stick butter
salt and pepper to taste

1. Carefully wash zucchini to remove all traces of sand.
2. With food processor or hand grater shred zucchini and sprinkle with kosher salt, and with a dish towel wring water from zucchini.
3. Mince shallots and garlic.
4. Heat large skillet, add oil then butter.
5. On a medium-high heat sauté garlic and shallots, adding zucchini, and stir-fry 4 to 5 minutes.
6. Add salt and pepper to taste.

## Creamy Italian Dressing

INGREDIENTS:

3 cups olive oil
¾ cup rice or wine vinegar
2 cloves garlic
  juice of one lemon
1 teaspoon oregano
1 teaspoon basil
1 tablespoon anchovy paste
1 raw egg
2 tablespoons Dijon mustard
  salt and pepper to taste
1 pint buttermilk

1. Combine all ingredients except oil and buttermilk into blender and stir on a low speed.
2. Turn to high speed and with motor running pour oil through lid hole slowly, until the dressing has reached a thin mayonnaise consistency, then add buttermilk.
3. Store in refrigerator.

(Recipe must be made twice.)

## Kahlua Hazelnut Torte

*Yield: 30 slices*

INGREDIENTS:

1 cup sugar
4 egg yolks
1 teaspoon vanilla
1 cup chopped hazelnuts
1 cup breadcrumbs
1 teaspoon baking powder
4 egg whites
½ cup Kahlua
1 cup heavy cream
1 teaspoon instant espresso or coffee
2 tablespoons sugar or honey (to be added to heavy cream)

1. Preheat oven to 375°.
2. Cream sugar and egg yolk.
3. Add vanilla, hazelnuts (reserve a few for garnish), breadcrumbs, baking powder. Mix thoroughly.
4. Whip egg whites until they stand in soft peaks.
5. Fold whites into torte mixture until evenly combined.
6. Grease loaf pan and flour lightly. Turn mixtures into pan and bake for 25 minutes.
7. Watch closely: torte is done when top is firm and dry to touch.
8. Cool on racks; invert onto serving plate or platter.
9. Make several punctures with a knife and drip Kahlua over torte.
10. Whip cream and add one teaspoon instant espresso and sugar or honey to sweeten slightly. Spread over torte or pipe on with pastry tube.
11. Sprinkle chopped hazelnuts on top of completed torte for garnish and refrigerate. Also, this freezes well.

Chapter 5

# A Sweet Sixteen Party for 25: Tempura Your Own!

IT HAPPENS ALL of a sudden. . . . One day you look up and that little girl with skinned knees is wearing lipstick and asking for the car keys: you've now got a young lady in the family!

There is no better time to celebrate her changes than on her Sweet Sixteen birthday, and we've got the party of the year ready for you to surprise her with.

The food flavors are peanutty and delicious and in view of that new independence, the menu features a "tempura bar" where her guests are invited to prepare their own tempura. Even dessert is especially fun, with a "Help Yourself" fruit fondue that features a caramel and chocolate dip.

The lady of the day will be the guest of honor at a star party she'll remember the rest of her life.

## A SWEET SIXTEEN PARTY FOR 25

# *Menu*

**DINNER BUFFET**

*Sesame Chicken with Cantaloupe*
*Tempura Your Own!*
*(a combination vegetable-shrimp tempura bar)*
*Sweet and Sour Sauce*
*Ginger-Scallion Tamari Dip*
*Tahini Noodle Salad*

**DESSERT**

*Fresh Fruit Fondue with*
*Caramel Sauce and Chocolate Dip*

*Pink Champagne Punch*

# Total Grocery List

**Produce:** 
2 large ripe cantaloupes
2 heads broccoli
1 head cauliflower
1 pound large carrots
4 large zucchini
4 large yellow squash
4 large sweet potatoes
3 bunches scallions

1 2-inch piece ginger root
4 pints strawberries
6 Bartlett pears
6 apples
1 ripe pineapple
4 navel oranges
1 garlic bulb

NOTE: Any firm, ripe seasonal fruit for fondue can be added.

**Dry Goods:**
1 quart soy sauce or tamari*
honey
Dijon mustard
sesame oil
3 quarts peanut oil
1 pound bag sesame seeds
5 pound bag flour
paprika
salt
parsley flakes
ginger powder
ground nutmeg
ground pepper

baking powder
1 16-ounce jar marmalade
1 container orange juice
rice vinegar
4 8-ounce bags semisweet chocolate bits
2 pounds caramel pieces
tahini sesame paste†
1 small bottle hot sesame oil
4 1-pound packages thin vermicelli pasta
1 jar chunky peanut butter
1 quart vegetable oil

**Poultry and Fish:**
5 pounds boneless breast of chicken
4 pounds medium-large shrimp

**Dairy:**
1 pound butter
1 dozen eggs

* Tamari is a naturally pressed soy sauce; it's very delicious and found in your natural food store.
† Tahini is made from ground sesame seeds and can be found in your natural food store.

|          |                                      |                                       |
|----------|--------------------------------------|---------------------------------------|
| *Beverage:* | 1 quart orange juice              | 2 bottles champagne                   |
|          | 4 12-ounce cans beer (for cooking)   | 2 quart bottles cranberry juice       |
|          | 4 bottles club soda                  | 1 5-pound block ice                   |
|          | 4 bottles ginger ale                 |                                       |
|          |                                      |                                       |
| *Special Equip-ment:* | 200 wooden skewers      | trays                                 |
|          | large punch bowl                     | portable electric burner and wok, or  |
|          | wok or baby fryer (for tempura)      |    electric wok, or electric deep fryer |
|          | double boiler                        |                                       |

## Party Plans

Our party is scheduled for a Saturday night at 8:00 P.M. and takes only the day before to prepare for.

**Friday**

a. Shop for Complete Grocery List.

b. Prepare chicken (recipe page 76), to step 5. Refrigerate tightly covered.

c. Prepare Sweet and Sour Sauce and Ginger-Scallion Tamari Dip (see recipes, page 78). Refrigerate covered.

d. Prepare tempura batter (page 77), refrigerate covered.

## Day of the Party

**Saturday**

NOON  Prepare vegetables and shrimp for tempura bar (see recipe, page 76). Refrigerate.

2:00 P.M.  Prepare Tahini Noodle Salad (see page 78). Refrigerate covered.

3:30 P.M.  Assemble Sesame Chicken with Cantaloupe, steps 6 to 8, page 76. Refrigerate.

4:30 P.M.  Prepare fruit for fondue (see recipe on page 78). Squeeze lemon over fruit to keep it from browning. Refrigerate.

5:30 P.M.*  Set up serving table and bar area.

6:30 P.M.  Relax and get dressed.

7:30 P.M.  Prepare punch (see page 79). Prepare dips for fondue (page 79).

8:00 P.M.  a. Greet guests, have them help themselves to punch.

b. Put out Sesame Chicken with Cantaloupe as appetizer.

8:45 P.M.  a. Start oil heating in wok.

b. Place vegetables and shrimp on serving trays, place on table.

c. Place dips on table.

9:00 P.M.  a. Start tempura bar.

b. Place Tahini Noodle Salad on table.

10:00 P.M. or whenever dinner is over  Heat up fondue dips in double boilers on stove, transfer to fondue pots, place fruit on platters. Place on serving table. Enjoy the fun!

* Set up wok over single portable electric burner or electric deep fryer or electric wok in center of table.

# Recipes

## Sesame Chicken with Cantaloupe

INGREDIENTS:

5 pounds boneless breast of chicken
¼ cup butter (1 stick)
¼ cup soy sauce
1 cup honey
1 tablespoon Dijon mustard
1 tablespoon sesame oil
1 egg (room temp.)
1 cup peanut oil
2 large ripe cantaloupes
1 pound sesame seeds
1 package of 100 skewers

1. Cut raw chicken into large bite-size pieces.
2. In skillet, melt 2 tablespoons butter, sauté chicken a bit at a time, adding more butter with each batch sauteed. Drain and let cool.
3. In blender jar, add soy sauce, honey, mustard, sesame oil, and egg; blend 10 seconds.
4. While blender motor is running, add peanut oil.
5. Pour blender mixture over chicken and let stand in refrigerator at least 2 hours, stirring occasionally.
6. Peel and cut cantaloupe into large bite-size chunks.
7. Skewer one chunk of cantaloupe and then add 1 piece chicken.
8. Put sesame seeds in a bowl, dip chicken end of skewer into bowl of seeds; refrigerate.

## Tempura Your Own!

(a combination vegetable-shrimp tempura bar)

INGREDIENTS:

4 pounds medium to large shrimp
2 heads broccoli
1 head cauliflower
1 pound large carrots
4 large zucchini
4 large yellow summer squash
4 large sweet potatoes
2 quarts peanut oil for deep-frying

1. Peel and clean shrimp—and butterfly by cutting lengthwise three quarters of the way toward tail. Wrap in plastic wrap and refrigerate.
2. Prepare vegetables as you would for Crudités (see page 195).
3. Prepare Batter.

### *Batter*

INGREDIENTS:

    3 eggs
    ¼ cup peanut oil
    4 cups flour
    4 12-ounce cans beer
    2 teaspoons paprika
    1 tablespoon salt
    4 tablespoons parsley flakes
    2 teaspoons ginger powder
    ½ teaspoon ground nutmeg
    1 teaspoon fresh ground pepper
    2 teaspoons baking powder

1. Beat eggs into oil.
2. Add 1 cup flour, mix thoroughly.
3. Add 1 can beer.
4. Continue adding flour and beer alternately.
5. Stir in remaining ingredients.
6. Cover and refrigerate.

NOTE: TIPS ON TEMPURA

1. It's important to keep batter very cold. An easy way to do this is to put bowl with batter inside a larger bowl filled with ice and water while in refrigerator and on serving table.
2. Place bowl of batter on one side of wok or fryer with tray of vegetables. Place dips on the other side.
3. Dip the vegetables one at a time in batter. Let drain a moment when lifting out and then place in oil a few at a time so that heat level does not drop. Turn once in oil and remove when golden. Place on paper toweling to drain.
4. Be sure to demonstrate this process to your guests before letting them take over.

**Sweet and Sour Sauce**

INGREDIENTS:

1 16-ounce jar orange marmalade
1 8-ounce cup orange juice
1 tablespoon soy sauce
1 cup rice vinegar
1 teaspoon ginger powder

Mix all ingredients thoroughly and refrigerate.

**Ginger-Scallion Tamari Dip**

INGREDIENTS:

3 scallions
1 2-inch piece ginger root
2 cups tamari or soy sauce
⅛ cup water

1. Mince scallions finely, place in medium size bowl.
2. Mince ginger root finely, add to bowl.
3. Add rest of ingredients.
4. Refrigerate covered for as long as possible (2 to 6 hours) before serving.

**Tahini Noodle Salad**

INGREDIENTS:

4 1-pound packages thin vermicelli pasta
2 bunches scallions minced
3 cloves garlic finely minced
2 tablespoons sesame oil, hot
1 cup peanut oil
2 cups tahini sesame paste
¼ cup tamari or soy sauce
1 cup chunky peanut butter

1. Cook noodles according to directions.
2. Sauté scallions and garlic in sesame and peanut oil. Remove from heat, mix in remaining ingredients.
3. Drain noodles, top with sauce; refrigerate.

**Fresh Fruit Fondue**

INGREDIENTS:

2 pints strawberries, brushed clean
6 Bartlett pears, cored and wedged
6 apples, cored and wedged
1 ripe pineapple, peeled, cored, and cut into chunks
4 navel oranges, peeled and separated, or any firm ripe seasonal fruit

Wooden skewers or fondue forks for 25

### Chocolate Dip

INGREDIENTS:

    4 8-ounce bags semisweet chocolate bits
    8 tablespoons vegetable oil

1. In double boiler melt chocolate with oil.
2. Transfer to fondue pot over low flame, stirring occasionally.

### Caramel Sauce

INGREDIENTS:

    2 pounds caramel pieces
    1 stick (¼ pound) butter

1. In double boiler melt caramel pieces with butter.
2. Transfer to fondue pot over low flame, stirring occasionally.

### Pink Champagne Punch

INGREDIENTS:

    4 bottles club soda
    8 bottles ginger ale
    2 bottles champagne
    2 quart bottles cranberry juice
    2 pints fresh strawberries, brushed clean and destemmed
    1 5-pound block ice

1. Combine half of all ingredients in large punch bowl just before serving.
2. Refill punch bowl when needed with remaining ingredients.

Chapter 6

# A Graduation Party for 35: Mexicana Olé!

WHEN IT'S TIME for a graduation party, it's time for Mexicana Olé!

For that very special occasion, you can create a specialty party that won't soon be forgotten. Our original Mexican menu starts off with tacos and is topped with Mexican beer. A Perfect Party for young adults, and you will handle thirty-five guests with ease.

Our time schedule is set for a Friday night graduation—for our purposes an hour-long ceremony at 7:00 P.M.—and is specially arranged so that you can attend the ceremony as well as cater your own affair.

No matter where you live—

Here comes a little bit of Mexico!

## GRADUATION PARTY FOR 35

# *Menu*

**ENTRÉES**

*Avocado Tacos with Hot Sauce*
*Seviche in Corn Husks*
*Chili con Carne and Corn Pie*

**ACCOMPANIMENT**

*Green Rice*

**DESSERT**

*Fresh Fruit Salad Supreme*

*Mexican Beer*

# Complete Grocery List

**Produce:**
3 pounds fresh asparagus
2 heads iceberg lettuce
8 very ripe avocados
2 lemons
2 bunches scallions
garlic bulb
1 bunch fresh dill
1 bunch fresh watercress
1 bunch parsley
6 limes

2 large red Bermuda onions
4 large onions
2 green peppers
1 dozen apples
1 dozen oranges
6 grapefruit
2 pounds seedless grapes
2 ripe melons
1 ripe pineapple, or 2 large cans pineapple chunks

**Dry Goods:**
70 packaged taco shells
Tabasco sauce
Worcestershire sauce
white pepper
salt
baking powder
Quaker cornmeal
1 small bag flour
1 8-ounce can tomato sauce with herbs
Dijon mustard
1 small bottle olive oil
1 quart peanut oil

1 tube anchovy paste
4 large cans whole peeled tomatoes
2 large cans tomato paste
1 package corn husks*
4 large cans pitted black olives
1 large can chili powder
1 small can ground cumin
1 large can or jar parsley flakes
1 small jar Jalapeño peppers
4 pounds white long grain rice
2 13½-ounce cans chicken stock
1 small bottle rice or wine vinegar
1 pound sugar

**Meat and Fish:**
1 pound bacon
8 pounds ground sirloin
5 pounds fillet of sole or flounder
3 pounds medium-size peeled, cleaned shrimp

* Corn Husks can be obtained from a Spanish-American grocery store or write to Casa Moneo Spanish Imports, 210 West 14th Street, New York, N.Y. 10011.

| | |
|---|---|
| *Frozen:* | 2 packages whole kernel corn |
| *Dairy:* | 3 pounds Monterey Jack cheese |
| | ½ pint sour cream |
| | 1 small jar mayonnaise |
| | 1 dozen eggs |
| | 1 quart milk |
| *Liquor:* | 5 cases Mexican beer |
| | 1 pint Triple Sec |
| | 50 pounds of ice |
| *Paper Goods:* | 4 dozen large paper dinner plates |
| | 4 dozen plastic spoons |
| | 4 dozen plastic forks |
| | 4 dozen plastic bowls (4 to 6 ounce) |
| |    for Fresh Fruit Salad Supreme) |
| | napkins |
| *Special Equipment:* | 8–10-quart pot (for Chili con Carne) |
| | blender |
| | 4 aluminum baking pans |
| | extra beer can opener |
| *Optional:* | flowers for decorating table |
| | 2 baskets for serving (1 large, |
| |    1 medium) |

## Party Plans

### Day of the Party

The party schedule is written according to a Friday night graduation party at 8:30 P.M., but can be easily adjusted to serve any day of the week.

This party for thirty-five is so simple to prepare, for you can begin preparation on the Wednesday before the party.

### Wednesday

a. Shop for ingredients. The Complete Grocery List can be purchased at this time.
b. Prepare Seviche in Corn Husks. See recipe, pages 88–89.

### Thursday

a. Prepare Chili con Carne and Corn Pie. See recipe, page 90.
b. Prepare Green Rice. See recipe, page 91.

### Friday

If you work a nine to five job, this Friday would be the day to take off!

NOON   Prepare Avocado Tacos with Hot Sauce. See recipe page 88.

2:00 P.M.   Stuff corn husks with Seviche, arrange in baskets or on trays, and refrigerate.

4:00 P.M.   Set up serving table. Prepare house for company. Set tables, arrange flowers.

5:00 P.M.   Fill tub with ice and chill beer.

6:00 P.M.   Relax, bathe, get ready for ceremony.

7:00–8:00 P.M.   Enjoy the ceremony.

8:30 P.M.   Start the party with Mexican beer. Put can openers nearby and let the people serve themselves. Return to the kitchen.

    a. Put Chili con Carne into 375° oven right from the refrigerator for ½ hour.
    b. Take Avocado Tacos out of aluminum trays and arrange in basket. Place on a serving table with Hot Sauce.
    c. Place bowl of Green Rice on serving table.
    d. Place Seviche husks in basket or trays on serving table.
    e. Chili con Carne should now be ready. Take directly from oven and place on serving table.
    f. The party food is ready: Enjoy! Let everybody help themselves.
    g. After dinner clear the table and bring out the Fresh Fruit Salad Supreme.
    h. *Congratulate yourself—you did it!*

## Recipes

### Avocado Tacos with Hot Sauce

*Yield: 70 tacos*

*Filling*

INGREDIENTS:

    8 very ripe avocados (soft to the touch)
        juice of 2 lemons*
    ½ teaspoon Tabasco
    1 tablespoon Worcestershire
    2 bunches scallions, finely minced
    2 cloves garlic, pressed
    ½ cup sour cream
    ½ cup mayonnaise
    ½ teaspoon white pepper
    1 teaspoon salt

*Tacos*

INGREDIENTS:

    70 taco shells (sold in boxes ready-made, or frozen, to be
        baked according to box directions)
    2 heads iceberg lettuce, shredded
    3 pounds shredded Monterey Jack cheese

*Hot Sauce*

INGREDIENTS:

    1 8-ounce can tomato sauce with herbs
    ¼ teaspoon Tabasco, or to taste
    ½ cup water

1. Mash avocados in large bowl.
2. Add all filling ingredients and combine well.
3. Fill taco shells half full with avocado mixture.
4. Sprinkle with shredded lettuce (about ¼ cup for each taco).
5. Top with shredded cheese (also about ¼ cup for each taco).
6. Place filled tacos upright in an aluminum roasting pan, cover with foil, and refrigerate.
7. Combine tomato sauce, Tabasco, and water in small bowl and refrigerate. This will be served on the side in a small bowl on the serving table.

* Save peel for zest in Fresh Fruit Salad Supreme; store in Ziploc bags.

### Seviche in Corn Husks

*Yield: Approximately 40*

INGREDIENTS:

    5 pounds fillet of sole, or any delicate thin fish, such as
        flounder
    1 bunch fresh dill, or 1 tablespoon dried dill
        juice of 6 limes*
    3 pounds peeled and cleaned medium-sized shrimp
    3 pounds fresh asparagus
    2 tablespoons Dijon mustard

1 clove garlic
1 tablespoon anchovy paste
1 egg
¼ teaspoon Tabasco
1 tablespoon Worcestershire sauce
½ teaspoon salt
½ teaspoon white pepper
¼ cup olive oil
1 cup peanut oil
2 large red Bermuda onions
1 package corn husks for serving

1. Cut raw fillets into thin strips (discarding bones if any).
2. Remove stems from dill and chop coarsely.
3. Combine lime juice with dill and fillet strips in glass or ceramic bowl. Cover tightly and place in refrigerator to marinate overnight or for at least 12 hours. Occasionally remove from refrigerator and stir to be sure all fillet strips are covered with the marinade. (The fish is actually being cooked by the acid in the lime juice.)
4. Next, plunge cleaned shrimp into boiling water until opaque (about 3 minutes). Drain and then cool in cold water. Set aside.
5. Rinse asparagus in cool water, and then cut the tops off (about 2 inches).
6. Plunge in boiling water to blanch (about 3 minutes). Drain and cool.
7. At this point the shrimp and asparagus can be covered and refrigerated until fish has been marinated 12 hours or overnight.
8. Drain ½ cup lime juice from fillets into blender.
9. Add mustard, garlic, anchovy paste, egg, Tabasco, Worcestershire, salt and pepper. Blend at high speed for 10 seconds.
10. Drizzle in the peanut and olive oil—either through the hole in your blender cover at high speed, or with the cover off and the speed at a lower setting.
11. Dice onions and toss with drained shrimp, asparagus, and fish.
12. Add sauce from blender and mix well.
13. Prepare corn husks by soaking them in boiling water, covered, for 10 minutes. Then turn off heat and remove husks one at a time. Fill each with ½ cup Seviche. Take 1 husk and tear into very thin strips about ⅛ inch wide. Use these strips to tie around twisted ends of filled husks.

* Save peel for zest in Fruit Salad Supreme; store in Ziploc bags.

## Chili Con Carne and Corn Pie

*Filling*

INGREDIENTS:

1 pound bacon
¼ cup olive oil
4 large onions, minced
8 pounds ground sirloin
6 tablespoons chili powder
8 tablespoons parsley flakes
2 cloves garlic, finely minced
1 teaspoon white pepper
1 teaspoon salt, or to taste
1 tablespoon ground cumin
4 large cans whole peeled tomatoes
2 large cans tomato paste
4 large cans ripe pitted olives
1 small jar Jalapeño peppers
2 packages frozen whole kernel corn

*Corn Bread Topping*

(You will need to make this recipe two times.) Follow recipe on Quaker cornmeal box.* Cover pie with mixture. Be sure to pour while mixture is loose and easy to spread.

1. Preheat oven to 375°.
2. Leave bacon unseparated and slice while still cold into ¼-inch strips vertically.
3. In your largest pot (8 to 10 quarts), sauté bacon and onion in olive oil. Stir the bacon well; it will separate into little pieces. Cook until bacon is crisp.
4. Add ground sirloin, stirring well over medium-high heat.
5. When the meat is no longer pink add the chili powder, parsley flakes, minced garlic, white pepper, salt, and cumin. Stir well.
6. Add tomatoes, squeezing in your hand before adding to pot.
7. Add tomato paste. Stir well; simmer over lower heat 45 minutes.
8. Slice olives. Set aside.
9. Mince 6 peppers finely, add to olives.
10. After Chili con Carne has cooked 45 minutes, stir in olives and peppers and corn. Turn off heat.
11. Place Chili con Carne into two large aluminum baking pans.
12. Prepare cornmeal mixture and top chili con carne, spreading thinly over the top of each pan.
13. Bake for 45 minutes, or until corn bread is golden and firm to touch.

* Ingredients for corn bread topping are included in your complete bakery list.

## Green Rice

INGREDIENTS:

7 cups white long grain rice
2 13½-ounce cans chicken stock
10½ cups water
2 teaspoons salt
1 cup plus 2 tablespoons peanut oil
2 cloves garlic, peeled
1 bunch watercress, chopped
1 bunch parsley, chopped
¼ cup rice or wine vinegar
½ teaspoon white pepper
2 green peppers, finely minced

1. In a 6-quart pot combine rice, stock, water, 1½ teaspoons salt and 2 tablespoons oil. Bring to boil. Cover and simmer 17 minutes, stirring occasionally. Remove from heat. Transfer to large flat aluminum roasting pan so that it will cook quickly and not become sticky.
2. In blender combine rest of ingredients except green peppers. Blend at high speed for 30 seconds.
3. Add finely minced peppers and liquid in blender to rice. When cool toss to combine well.
4. Place in large wooden bowl, cover, and refrigerate.

## Fresh Fruit
## Salad Supreme

*Fruit*

INGREDIENTS:

1 dozen oranges
1 dozen apples
6 grapefruit
2 pounds seedless grapes
2 ripe melons (cantaloupe or honeydew)
1 ripe fresh pineapple, or 2 large cans pineapple chunks

1. Cut the top and bottom off oranges and peel them. Slice into rounds ¼ inch thick. Put into large bowl.
2. Quarter and core apples. Leave skin on and cut into chunks. Add to bowl.
3. Peel grapefruit and cut into chunks. Add to bowl.
4. Remove grapes from stem; if large, cut into halves. Add to bowl.
5. Peel and clean melons, cut into chunks. Add to bowl.
6. Peel and core pineapple (if fresh), cut into chunks. If canned, drain. Add to bowl. Set aside.
7. Prepare sauce.

*Sauce*

INGREDIENTS:

zest* of 2 limes, 2 lemons, and 1 orange
1 cup sugar
1 cup water
½ cup Triple Sec

1. In heavy 2-quart saucepan, combine all sauce ingredients. Bring to boil over medium heat, stirring occasionally until it comes to a syrupy consistency. Cool.
2. Pour over fruit, toss, and refrigerate, tightly covered, in serving bowl.

\* The term "zest" refers to the outer rind of the fruit. It is obtained by peeling the outer layer off with a potato peeler.

Chapter 7

# Outdoor Fun for 8: A Picnic for the Country or the City

TAKE IT TO the beach or out to the country! Here's a feast for the road that eight people will never forget. . . .

## OUTDOOR FUN FOR 8

# *Menu*

**ENTRÉE**

*Tomato Baskets with Curried Shrimp
Artichokes with Lemon Mustard Vinaigrette
Blue Cheese Potato Salad*

**DESSERT**

*Lemon Mousse*

*Champagne*

# Complete Grocery List

**Produce:** 1 small head red cabbage  
4 lemons  
8 tomatoes  
1 bunch fresh dill  
6 medium to large potatoes  

1 large Bermuda onion  
1 bunch celery  
2 bunches parsley  
8 large artichokes  
1 bulb garlic  

**Dry Goods:** 1 small bag sugar  
1 4-ounce can water chestnuts  
Worcestershire sauce  
olive oil  
peanut oil  
curry powder  
1 tube anchovy paste  
dill  
Dijon mustard  
black and white pepper  
soy sauce or tamari  

1 4-ounce jar olives with pimentos  
1 4-ounce jar gherkins  
salt  
rice or wine vinegar  
celery salt  
1 pint mayonnaise  
1 bag sesame seeds (optional)  
1 package gelatin  
A.1. sauce  
lemon crisp  

**Fish:** 3 pounds peeled, cleaned shrimp  

**Frozen:** 1 can condensed lemonade  

**Dairy:** 2 dozen eggs  
¼ pound blue cheese  

1 pint sour cream  
1 pint heavy cream  

**Liquor:** 1 pint dark rum  
5 bottles champagne  

**Paper Goods:** 20 paper plates  
20 napkins  
20 plastic knives, forks, spoons  

20 plastic cups  
plastic wrap  
aluminum foil  

**Additional:** picnic basket  
cardboard carton  

**Special Equipment:** blender

## Party Plans

**Two Days Before**

Shop for all ingredients and prepare Artichokes with Lemon Mustard Vinaigrette (page 101) and Lemon Mousse (see recipe, page 103).

**The Night Before**

Prepare Tomato Baskets with Curried Shrimp (see recipe, page 100) and Blue Cheese Potato Salad (page 102). Be sure to chill the champagne.

## Day of the Party

**That Morning**

Pack it all up and head for the picnic of your life!

# Recipes

## Tomato Baskets with Curried Shrimp

INGREDIENTS:

3 pounds peeled, cleaned shrimp
1 4-ounce can sliced water chestnuts
2 cups shredded red cabbage
8 large ripe tomatoes
1 tablespoon Worcestershire sauce
2 eggs
½ cup olive oil
1 cup peanut oil
2 tablespoons lemon juice
1 tablespoon curry powder
1 tablespoon anchovy paste
1 tablespoon dried dill or 2 tablespoons fresh chopped dill
1 tablespoon Dijon mustard
½ teaspoon white pepper
1 tablespoon soy sauce
1 small bunch fresh dill (for garnish)

1. Drop peeled and cleaned shrimp into boiling water until shrimp becomes opaque (about 3 minutes).
2. In a blender combine all ingredients except shrimp, water chestnuts, cabbage, and tomatoes. Blend for 5 seconds at high speed.
3. Chop shrimp into large coarse pieces.
4. Toss all ingredients together except tomatoes.
5. Cut tomatoes into baskets (see illustration).
6. Stuff shrimp mixture into baskets. Garnish with fresh dill and refrigerate.

## *Artichokes with Lemon Mustard Vinaigrette*

INGREDIENTS:

8 large artichokes
1 clove garlic, pressed
3 tablespoons lemon juice
2 tablespoons Dijon mustard
1 tablespoon A.1. sauce
½ cup olive oil
1 cup peanut oil
1 tablespoon chopped parsley
2 hard-boiled eggs
¼ teaspoon salt
¼ teaspoon pepper
1 teaspoon sugar

1. Debarb the artichokes (see illustration). Trim bottom to stand up straight.
2. Boil artichokes in salted water until tender (about 35 minutes). Remove from heat; turn artichokes upside down to drain. Let cool. Refrigerate wrapped in plastic.
3. In stainless steel bowl, whisk garlic, lemon juice, mustard, and A.1. sauce until combined.
4. While whisking mixture, drizzle in olive and peanut oil *slowly*.
5. When mixture becomes creamy in texture, add chopped parsley, eggs, salt, and pepper.
6. Pour in jar with tight-fitting lid. Refrigerate.

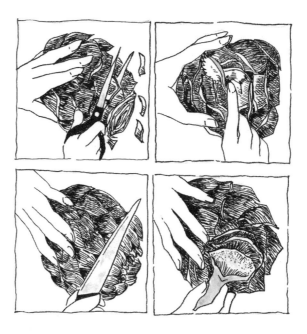

**INGREDIENTS:**

## Blue Cheese
## Potato Salad

6 medium to large potatoes, scrubbed well
1 large red Bermuda onion
1 4-ounce jar gherkins
4 stalks celery
1 4-ounce jar olives with pimentos
1 bunch parsley
6 hard-boiled eggs
4 ounces blue cheese
¼ cup rice or wine vinegar
1½ tablespoons Dijon mustard
2 teaspoons salt
½ teaspoon celery salt
2 cups mayonnaise (homemade if possible)
1 tablespoon anchovy paste
½ pint sour cream
½ cup sesame seeds (optional)

1. Dice potatoes, unpeeled, into large pot of cold, unsalted water.
2. Boil potatoes until tender, drain, and rinse under cold water.
3. Peel and slice onion into paper-thin slices.
4. Slice gherkins thinly.
5. Chop celery finely.
6. Slice olives.
7. Chop parsley.
8. Chop hard-boiled eggs coarsely.
9. In medium bowl combine blue cheese and vinegar and mash into paste.
10. Add mustard, spices, oil, mayonnaise, anchovy paste, and sour cream and mix. Add sesame seeds if using. When thoroughly combined, add all ingredients together in large bowl. Mix well and refrigerate.

## Lemon Mousse

INGREDIENTS:

¼ cup dark rum
1 can condensed lemonade
  juice of one lemon
  grated zest (peel) of 2 lemons
1 package gelatin
6 eggs
1 pint heavy cream, whipped
¼ teaspoon salt
  Optional: Serve with Lemon Crisp boxed cookies

1. Heat rum, undiluted lemonade, lemon juice, zest, and gelatin over low heat, stirring until gelatin is dissolved.
2. Separate eggs.
3. In large bowl, combine yolks with lemon mixture. Stir well.
4. Beat egg whites with salt until soft peaks form.
5. Fold in whipped cream to lemon mixture.
6. Gently fold in beaten egg whites.
7. Pour into individual plastic cups and top with plastic wrap. Refrigerate.
8. Serve with cookies, if desired.

Chapter 8

# An Office Party for 25 to 30: You're Chef of the Office!

HERE IT IS—your time to shine as the chef of the office! If it seems a bit too much of an undertaking for you, you can enlist some helpers and have them make a recipe at home and bring it in. Whichever way you do it—you're sure to be an office star on party day!

*AN OFFICE PARTY FOR 25 TO 30*

# *Menu*

*Crudités with Caesar Dip*
*Chicken Roulades*
*Gorgonzola Spinach Mushrooms*
*Three Cheese Pita*
*Tapenade Pinwheels*
*Sausage Quiche Squares*

*Full Bar*

# *Full Bar Guide* *

*Liquor:*  3 quarts vodka
2 quarts Scotch
1 quart gin
1 quart bourbon
1 quart rye
6 bottles or 2 magnums white wine
1 pint dry vermouth
1 quart white rum

*Mixers:*  2 quarts club soda
4 quarts mineral water
2 quarts orange juice
3 quarts tonic
2 quarts Coke
2 quarts ginger ale
1 bottle Bloody Mary mix
1 bottle lime juice
1 small jar cocktail olives
20 pounds ice (have delivered
    directly to office, if possible)
1 small jar cocktail onions
4 limes
2 lemons

* Check with people in office to see what they prefer and adjust accordingly.

# Complete Grocery List

**Produce:** 3 pounds fresh medium to large
      mushrooms
1 large garlic bulb
1 large and 1 small onion
2 bunches watercress
2 bunches parsley
1 head cauliflower
1 head broccoli
1 pound green beans

3 large zucchini
3 large summer squash
1 pound large carrots
2 large cucumbers
1 head cabbage (red, if possible)
1 bunch scallions
1 box cherry tomatoes
5 lemons
4 limes

**Dry
Goods:** 1 quart red wine vinegar
1 pint rice vinegar or red wine
      vinegar
1 pint olive oil
2 medium cans tuna
1 large jar pearl cocktail onions
Dijon mustard
Worcestershire sauce
salt
white pepper
lemon pepper
basil
parsley flakes

garlic powder
1 tube anchovy paste
1 can chicken broth
1 can anchovies with capers, in oil
1 quart peanut oil
1 quart vegetable oil
1 five-pound bag white flour,
      unbleached
4 packages pita bread (4 to 6 to a
      package)
1 pound Greek black olives
1 small jar cocktail olives
1 small jar onions

**Meat,
Poultry,
Fish:** 6 full boneless chicken breasts
2 pounds boiled ham
1 pound sweet Italian sausage

**Frozen:** 3 packages chopped spinach

**Dairy:** ¼ pound Gorgonzola cheese
4 pounds cottage cheese (large curd)
2 8-ounce packages cream cheese
2 4-ounce packages Alouette cheese
      with herbs or Boursin cheese
1 dozen eggs
2 sticks butter

1 pint half-and-half cream
¾ pound sharp Cheddar cheese
¾ pound Swiss cheese
¼ pound Parmesan cheese (fresh or
      in a jar)
1½ pounds Swiss cheese
1 package filo pastry

*Liquor:*  See Full Bar Guide, page 109.

*Paper*   100 cocktail napkins
*Goods:*  100 plastic cups

*Addi-*   7 trays for serving. We always use
*tional:*     big flat basket trays, which can be
          purchased inexpensively where
          available.
          flowers for tray garnish
          tablecloth for serving table
          ice bucket

## Party Plans

### The weekend before

Your party is scheduled for a Friday afternoon; the weekend before it would be a good idea to grocery shop for all your dry goods and all your Sausage Quiche ingredients.

GROCERY LIST

1 quart red wine vinegar
1 pint rice vinegar or red wine vinegar
1 pint olive oil
2 medium cans tuna fish
large jar pearl cocktail onions
Dijon mustard
Worcestershire sauce
salt
white pepper
lemon pepper
basil
parsley flakes
garlic powder
1 tube anchovy paste

1 can chicken broth
1 can anchovies with capers, in oil
1 quart peanut oil
1 quart vegetable oil
1 five-pound bag white flour, unbleached
1 dozen eggs
1 pint half-and-half cream
1 small onion
¾ pound sharp Cheddar cheese
¾ pound Swiss cheese
1 pound sweet Italian sausage
1 stick butter

### Monday evening

a. Prepare Sausage Quiche Squares (see recipe page 120). Cover tightly and refrigerate on cookie sheet.

### Tuesday day

Shop for several additional items.

GROCERY LIST

3 pounds mushrooms (medium to large size)
1 pound Greek black olives
garlic bulb
1 package filo pastry

### Tuesday evening

a. Marinate mushrooms (see recipe for Gorgonzola Spinach Mushrooms, page 118).
b. Prepare Tapenade Pinwheels (see page 119). Store in container with tight-fitting cover. No need to refrigerate.

### Wednesday day

Shop for these items:

¼ pound Gorgonzola cheese
1 large onion
3 packages frozen chopped spinach
6 full boneless chicken breasts
2 pounds boiled ham
1½ pounds Swiss cheese
2 bunches parsley
1 dozen eggs
1 stick butter
1 lemon
¼ pound Parmesan cheese

## Wednesday evening

a. Prepare Chicken Roulades (see recipe, page 117). Store in refrigerator, tightly covered.
b. Prepare Gorgonzola Spinach Mushrooms (page 118). Store in refrigerator, tightly covered.
c. Prepare Caesar Dip (see recipe, page 116). Store in tightly covered container and refrigerate.

## Thursday day

Pick up remaining groceries.

GROCERY LIST

4 pounds cottage cheese (large curd)
2 8-ounce packages cream cheese
2 4-ounce packages Alouette cheese with herbs, or Boursin cheese
2 bunches watercress
4 packages pita bread (4 to 6 to a pack)
1 head cauliflower
1 head broccoli
1 pound green beans
3 large zucchini
3 large summer squash
1 pound large carrots
2 large cucumbers
1 head cabbage (red, if possible)
1 bunch scallions
1 box cherry tomatoes
4 limes
1 small jar cocktail olives
1 small jar cocktail onions
5 lemons

## Thursday evening

a. Prepare Crudités (see recipe, page 116 and pages 195–197); store vegetables in Ziploc bags individually.
b. Prepare Three Cheese Pita. See recipe on page 118.

## Day of the Party

**Friday (before you leave for work)**

a. Cut pita into triangles, three pieces to each half. Place triangles on cookie sheet, cover with aluminum foil.

b. Cut Sausage Quiche into 96 squares (see illustration on page 34). Leave on cookie sheet, wrapped in aluminum foil.

c. Slice Chicken Roulades into ⅓-inch rounds. Put back into roll shape, wrap in aluminum foil.

d. Pack and take:

  tablecloth
  paper goods (napkins, cups)
  liquor, and ice if not delivered directly to office
  wine opener
  Crudités with Caesar Dip
  Chicken Roulades
  Three Cheese Pita
  skewers
  Tapenade Pinwheels
  Sausage Quiche
  Gorgonzola Spinach Mushrooms
  flowers for garnish, if using
  flat baskets or trays for serving
  spatula to remove quiche from cookie sheet

**Friday, at the office**

a. Refrigerate Caesar Dip, and Three Cheese Pita, if at all possible. Set up a table with tablecloth for serving.

b. Arrange Sausage Quiche Squares on tray and garnish with fresh flowers, if using. Place on serving table.

c. Arrange Chicken Roulades on tray and garnish with fresh flowers, if using. Place on serving table.

d. Arrange Crudités with cored-out cabbage head in center filled with the Caesar Dip. Place on serving table.

e. Place triangles of Three Cheese Pita on tray and garnish with fresh flowers, if using. Place on serving table.

f. Place Gorgonzola Spinach Mushrooms on tray, garnish with fresh flowers, if using. Place on serving table.

g. Arrange Tapenade Pinwheels on tray and put on serving table.

h. Set up bar on another table. Put out bottles, cups, and ice in bucket.

i. Put napkins on serving table at each end.

j. Go enjoy the party!

# Recipes

## Crudités with Caesar Dip

Crudités are an arrangement of beautiful fresh vegetables served with a dip. They are so eye-catching and such an important part of the party decor that we have devoted an entire section to them in chapter 15 on pages 195–197. Please refer to it now for this part of the Office Party recipes.

INGREDIENTS:

1 head cauliflower
1 head broccoli
1 pound green beans
3 large zucchini
3 large summer squash
1 pound large carrots
2 large cucumbers
1 head red cabbage
1 bunch scallions
1 box cherry tomatoes

### Caesar Dip

INGREDIENTS:

2 cups peanut oil
2 eggs
¼ pound fresh grated or bottled Parmesan cheese
2 tablespoons anchovy paste
2 tablespoons Worcestershire sauce
   juice of 1 lemon
½ teaspoon white pepper
2½ tablespoons parsley flakes, or 1 small bunch parsley
¼ cup rice vinegar
1 large garlic clove (peeled)
1 teaspoon Dijon mustard
½ cup olive oil
2 cups peanut oil

1. Place all ingredients except oils in blender jar. Blend at high speed 15 seconds.
2. Now drizzle oils through hole in lid, or remove top and with motor at low setting, pour in oils.
3. Dip will thicken as you add oil. Place in container; store tightly covered in refrigerator.

## Chicken Roulades

*Yield: Approximately 75 roulades*

**INGREDIENTS:**

6 full boneless chicken breasts, both sides of the breast left whole
2 pounds boiled ham
1½ pounds Swiss cheese
1 bunch parsley, finely chopped
4 eggs
¼ cup water
2 cups all-purpose flour
2 teaspoons garlic powder
2 teaspoons salt
1 teaspoon white pepper
4 tablespoons (½ stick) butter
½ cup vegetable oil

1. Remove the smaller strip of flesh from the underside of each breast and set aside (that strip is often referred to as the "mignon filet").
2. On a slightly wet cutting surface (or between 2 sheets of waxed paper) pound the breasts with a mallet or cleaver into a rectangle shape with about a ¼-inch thickness. If the chicken breasts you purchased were split, overlap the two sides by about 1 inch and pound together.
3. Cut the ham into julienne strips about ¼-inch wide. Set aside.
4. Shred the cheese. Set aside.
5. Divide the ham into 6 equal amounts and lay on center of each chicken breast.
6. Divide cheese into 6 equal parts. Lay on top of ham.
7. Divide chopped parsley in 6 equal parts and lay on top of cheese.
8. Roll the breasts up the long way. If any holes appear, patch with the mignons.
9. Refrigerate uncovered on a cookie sheet for 1 hour.
10. Beat eggs in a bowl with water.
11. Combine flour, garlic powder, salt, and pepper in another bowl.
12. Heat (slowly) butter and oil in skillet.
13. Dip rolls into egg, then flour mixture, and fry until golden.
14. Drain on paper towels.
15. Wrap in aluminum foil individually after cooling, and refrigerate.

## Gorgonzola Spinach Mushrooms

*Yield: Approximately 60 caps*

INGREDIENTS:

3 pounds medium to large fresh mushrooms
1 quart red wine vinegar
6 cloves garlic, peeled and minced
4 ounces Gorgonzola cheese
3 packages frozen chopped spinach
1 teaspoon white pepper
2 teaspoons salt, or to taste
1 large onion, finely minced
¼ cup olive oil
1 large jar pearl cocktail onions

1. Remove stems carefully from mushrooms. Rinse caps to remove any soil. Drain.
2. Place caps in a large bowl and pour 1 quart of wine vinegar over them.
3. Add garlic and let marinate at room temperature for 6 hours.
4. Put Gorgonzola cheese in a medium-size bowl.
5. Take ½ cup vinegar from marinating mushrooms and add to cheese.
6. Mash cheese and vinegar with fork until cheese is in small pieces.
7. Thaw spinach and squeeze out liquid.
8. Add spinach to cheese and vinegar with all remaining ingredients except pearl onions. Combine thoroughly.
9. Drain mushroom caps. Pat dry with paper towels.
10. Lay a double thickness of paper toweling on 2 cookie sheets.
11. Stuff caps with spinach-cheese mixture, put on cookie sheet and garnish each cap with one pearl onion.
12. Cover tightly with aluminum foil and refrigerate.

## Three Cheese Pita

INGREDIENTS:

4 pounds cottage cheese (large curd)
2 8-ounce packages cream cheese (softened)
2 4-ounce packages Alouette herb or Boursin cheese
1 tablespoon Worcestershire sauce
2 bunches watercress
4 packages pita bread (4 to 6 to a package)

1. In a large bowl, empty cottage cheese, add softened cream cheese, Alouette cheese, and 1 tablespoon Worcestershire. Blend together with wooden spoon.
2. Chop watercress finely (or use a food processor). Add to bowl and combine thoroughly.
3. Cut pita rounds in half and carefully open pocket.

4. Stuff with 3 tablespoons of cheese mixture.
5. Stack, wrap in foil, refrigerate.
6. Several hours before the party the pita halves will be cut into three triangles.

## Tapenade Pinwheels

*Yield: Approximately 60 pinwheels*

INGREDIENTS:

1 pound Greek black olives
2 medium cans tuna
1 can anchovies with capers, in oil
½ cup olive oil
6 large garlic cloves, peeled
1 package filo pastry

1. Preheat oven to 400°.
2. Remove the pits from the olives by pressing your thumb and forefinger together near the bottom of the olive.
3. Empty olives into blender jar or processor bowl (if using a blender, do a small amount at a time).
4, Puree olives and empty into bowl.
5. Add remaining ingredients except pastry into blender jar or processor bowl. Puree and add to bowl with olives.
6. Separate pastry leaves and spread a thick layer of the olive mixture on pastry.
7. Roll up pastry, starting with the small side of the rectangle.
8. Place in freezer for 15 minutes.
9. Remove from freezer and slice each roll into four pieces.
10. Place on greased cookie sheet and bake for 20 minutes or until pastry is golden brown.
11. Store pinwheels, after cooling, in a container and cover tightly.

## Sausage Quiche Squares

*Yield: 96 squares*

### Dough

INGREDIENTS:

2 cups white flour, unbleached
½ cup butter
½ teaspoon salt
5 tablespoons ice water

### Filling

INGREDIENTS:

1 pound sweet Italian sausage
2 tablespoons olive oil
7 large eggs
2 cups half-and-half cream
1 small onion
½ 13½-ounce can chicken broth
½ teaspoon salt
1 teaspoon lemon pepper (optional)
1 tablespoon Worcestershire sauce
1 teaspoon basil
3 tablespoons parsley flakes
1 large clove garlic
1½ cups shredded cheese (¾ cup sharp Cheddar, ¾ cup Swiss)

1. Prepare dough by blending first 3 ingredients until texture is crumbly. You can use a pastry blender or the knife and fork method.
2. Add 1 tablespoon of water at a time until dough pulls together.
3. Form into ball and refrigerate ½ hour.
4. Meanwhile preheat oven to 375° and prepare filling.
5. Remove sausage from wrappings and put into bowl.
6. Heat olive oil in skillet and add sausage. Stir until well cooked, breaking into a crumbly texture.
7. Drain sausage. Set aside.
8. In blender combine all filling ingredients except cheese and sausage.
9. Blend at high speed 30 seconds.
10. Take dough from refrigerator and roll out into a rectangle slightly larger than your cookie sheet. Transfer to cookie sheet.
11. Crimp edges of dough ¼ inch higher on sides than sheet to form a rim.
12. Lay cheese on dough, spreading evenly.
13. Put filling from blender on top of dough and cheese.
14. Top with sausage.
15. Bake for 45 minutes or until golden brown, then cool.
16. Store in refrigerator on cookie sheet, tightly wrapped.
17. Cut into 96 squares before serving. See illustration page 34.

## Chapter 9

# Christmas Stuffings for 12 to 15

THERE IS NO better time of year than Christmas for entertaining at home. This holiday dinner is an elegant and festive occasion that both you and your guests will remember well after the season has passed.

## CHRISTMAS STUFFINGS FOR 12 TO 15

# *Menu*

**APPETIZER**

*Seviche on Avocado Wings with
Smoked Salmon Rose Garnish*

**ENTRÉE**

*Stuffed Pork Chops with
Wild Rice, Pine Nuts, Apples, and Currants*

**VEGETABLES**

*Citrus-Glazed Cranberries
Broccoli with Hollandaise
Potatoes au Gratin*

**DESSERT**

*Chocolate Luv Cake*

*White Bordeaux Wine*

# Complete Grocery List

**Produce:** 1 bunch fresh or dry dill
4 limes
garlic bulb
4 avocados
1 box currants
¼ pound pine nuts
4 ounces toasted slivered almonds

3 cooking apples
1 orange
3 lemons
2 pounds fresh cranberries
6 pounds Idaho baking potatoes
2 pounds yellow onions
3 heads broccoli

**Dry Goods:** Dijon mustard
1 small bottle olive oil
1 bottle peanut oil
1 tube anchovy paste
Tabasco sauce
Worcestershire sauce
salt
white pepper
3 boxes semisweet Baker's chocolate
1 pound sugar

1 small bag flour
vanilla
2 pounds powdered sugar
coffee (instant or ground for ½ cup
in icing recipe)
24 ounces wild rice
cinnamon
paprika
parsley flakes

**Meat and Fish:** 2 pounds fresh fillet of sole or
flounder
2 pounds peeled, cleaned medium-
size shrimp

½ pound smoked salmon
20 large center-cut pork chops (with
slits for pockets

**Dairy:** 3 dozen eggs
3 pounds butter

1 pound sharp Cheddar cheese
1 quart milk

**Liquor:** 1 bottle applejack brandy
1 bottle Grand Marnier

1 bottle white wine
6 bottles white Bordeaux wine

**Special Equip-ment:** blender

## Party Plans

**Three days before Christmas**

a. Grocery shop for complete Grocery List items.
b. Prepare first four steps of Seviche recipe, page 128.

**Two days before Christmas**

Prepare Chocolate Luv Cake, both cake and icing (see recipe, pages 131–132). Refrigerate.

**One day before Christmas**

a. Stuff pork chops (see recipe, page 129). Refrigerate *uncooked* in baking pan tightly covered.
b. Prepare Citrus-Glazed Cranberries (see recipe, page 130). Refrigerate tightly covered.

## Day of the Party

**Christmas day—(dinner 6:00 P.M.)**

NOON    Complete Seviche recipe. Refrigerate. Do not assemble on plates yet.

1:00 P.M.    Prepare Potatoes au Gratin (see recipe, pages 130–131). Do not bake yet. Set aside.

2:30 P.M.    Set table.

3:00 P.M.    Prepare Broccoli with Hollandaise (see page 130).

4:00 P.M.    Assemble Seviche. Refrigerate plates with assembled Seviches on them.

4:15 P.M.    Preheat oven to 350°.

4:30 P.M.    Put Potatoes au Gratin in oven.

5:00 P.M.    Put pork chops in oven, and go get dressed!

6:00 P.M.    You're ready to go.

    a. Turn off oven and remove potatoes.
    b. Pop in broccoli to warm.
    c. Serve Seviche.
    d. After the appetizer is cleared, dinner is ready to go.
    e. Serve pork chops with Citrus-Glazed Cranberries, Broccoli with Hollandaise and Potatoes au Gratin.
    f. After dinner, clear and serve your Chocolate Luv Cake with pride!

# Recipes

*Seviche on
Avocado
Wings with
Smoked
Salmon Rose
Garnish*

*Seviche*

INGREDIENTS:

2 pounds fillet of sole, or any delicate thin fish such as
    flounder
1 bunch fresh dill, or 1 tablespoon dried dill
  juice of 4 limes*
2 pounds peeled, cleaned medium-sized shrimp
1 tablespoon Dijon mustard
1 clove garlic
1 teaspoon anchovy paste
1 egg at room temperature
¼ teaspoon Tabasco sauce
1 tablespoon Worcestershire sauce
½ teaspoon salt
½ teaspoon white pepper
½ cup peanut oil
⅛ cup olive oil

*Garnish*

INGREDIENTS:

4 avocados
½ pound smoked salmon

1. Cut raw fillets into thin strips (discarding bones if any).
2. Remove stems from fresh dill and chop coarsely.
3. Combine lime juice with dill and fillet strips in a glass or ceramic bowl. Cover tightly and place in refrigerator to marinate overnight, or for at least 12 hours. Occasionally remove from refrigerator and stir to be sure all fillet strips are covered with the marinade. (The fish is actually being cooked by the acid in the lime juice.)
4. Next plunge cleaned shrimp into boiling water until opaque (about 3 minutes). Drain and then cool in cold water. Leave shrimp in cold water and store in refrigerator tightly covered.
5. After fillets have marinated overnight or for at least 12 hours, drain ¾ cup lime juice from fillets into blender jar.
6. Add mustard, garlic, anchovy paste, egg, Tabasco, Worcestershire, salt and pepper. Blend at high speed for 10 seconds.
7. Drizzle in peanut and olive oil either through the hole in your blender cover at high speed, or with the cover off and the speed at a low setting.
8. Drain shrimp and toss together with blender sauce and fillets. Mix together well and then refrigerate tightly covered.
9. Prepare the Avocado Wings and Smoked Salmon Rose Garnish. (See illustrations.)

* Save peel for zest in Citrus-Glazed Cranberries. Store in Ziploc bags.

*Stuffed Pork
Chops with
Wild Rice,
Pine Nuts,
Apples, and
Currants*

INGREDIENTS:

20 large center-cut pork chops (ask butcher to cut pockets
    into chops for stuffing)
3 cups wild rice
3 cooking apples (such as Rome)
1 stick butter
⅔ cup currants
¼ pound pine nuts
2 eggs, slightly beaten
½ cup applejack brandy
1 teaspoon cinnamon
½ teaspoon salt
⅛ teaspoon pepper

1. Preheat oven to 350°.
2. Cook rice according to package directions.
3. Core and dice apples with skins left on.
4. Melt butter in small saucepan.
5. Combine in saucepan apples and remaining stuffing ingredients, except salt and pepper.
6. Open slits in pork chops and fill pockets with stuffing until chops bulge slightly. Place in baking dish.
7. Salt and pepper chops and cover with aluminum foil.
8. Bake covered for 35 minutes. Uncover and continue baking 15 minutes more. Total cooking time: 50 minutes.

## Citrus-Glazed Cranberries

INGREDIENTS:

1½ cups sugar
2 cups water
  zest* of 2 limes, 1 orange, 1 lemon
½ cup Grand Marnier
2 1-pound packages fresh cranberries, cleaned and
  destemmed

1. In a medium saucepan combine sugar and water and bring to
   a boil.
2. Cut zest* into thin julienne strips and add to saucepan.
3. Allow to boil 15 minutes over medium heat, or until mixture
   becomes a thin syrup.
4. Add ½ cup Grand Marnier.
5. Toss in cranberries. Cook for 3 minutes. Remove from heat
   and cool.

* "Zest" is the term for the outer skin of fruit. It is obtained using a potato
peeler and skinning the fruit.

## Broccoli with Hollandaise

INGREDIENTS:

3 heads broccoli
1 pound melted butter
3 tablespoons lemon juice*
½ teaspoon salt
8 egg yolks
½ teaspoon white pepper

1. Preheat oven to 350°.
2. Cut broccoli into spears, removing lower 2 inches of stem.
3. Melt butter in saucepan till hot and bubbly. Do not burn.
4. Add all ingredients except broccoli and butter to blender jar.
   Blend 5 seconds. With motor running pour in bubbly melted
   butter.
5. Blanch broccoli by plunging into boiling water for 3 minutes.
6. Arrange broccoli on ovenproof platter and pour Hollandaise
   over. Set aside.
7. Just before serving pop into oven for 10 minutes.

* Save lemon peel for zest of lemon in Citrus-Glazed Cranberries.

## Potatoes au Gratin

INGREDIENTS:

6 pounds Idaho baking potatoes
2 pounds yellow onions, sliced thinly into rounds
3 teaspoons salt
2 teaspoons white pepper
4 tablespoons parsley flakes
2 teaspoons paprika

½ stick (4 tablespoons) butter
3 tablespoons flour
3 cups milk
1 tablespoon Worcestershire sauce
2 cloves garlic, pressed
1 pound grated sharp Cheddar cheese
½ cup white wine

1. Preheat oven to 350°.
2. Scrub potatoes very well to remove all soil, and slice thinly, leaving skins on.
3. Push onion rounds in to form rings.
4. Grease 2 large casserole dishes. Put in a layer of sliced potatoes, sprinkle with some salt, white pepper, parsley flakes, and paprika. Top with a thin layer of onions.
5. Continue to layer and season, ending with top layer of potatoes.
6. In heavy 2-quart saucepan, melt butter, whisk in flour, stir and cook until light golden in color.
7. Whisk in milk. Continue whisking until sauce begins to thicken slightly.
8. Add Worcestershire sauce, garlic, shredded Cheddar cheese, and white wine.
9. When cheese has melted into sauce, pour over casseroles, letting sauce sink to bottom.
10. Bake 1½ hours, covered.
11. Remove foil for last 20 minutes to brown.

## Chocolate Luv Cake

INGREDIENTS:

2 boxes semisweet Baker's chocolate
4 sticks (1 pound) butter
1 dozen eggs, separated
1½ cups sugar
1 teaspoon salt
1 cup flour
2 teaspoons vanilla

1. Preheat oven to 375°.
2. In double boiler melt chocolate and add butter.
3. In large mixing bowl, mix egg yolks with sugar.
4. Whip egg whites with salt until soft peaks form.
5. Combine chocolate mixture with sugar mixture.
6. Stir in flour and vanilla, mixing thoroughly.
7. Gently fold in egg whites.
8. Pour into two 9-inch (greased and floured) round cake pans and bake 35 minutes, or until top forms a firm-to-the-touch crust.

## *Chocolate Luv Cake Icing*

INGREDIENTS:

6 squares semisweet Baker's chocolate
1 stick butter
½ cup hot coffee
4 egg yolks
6 cups powdered sugar
1 teaspoon vanilla
½ cup toasted slivered almonds

1. In a double boiler melt chocolate and butter.
2. Remove from stove, stir in coffee and let cool slightly.
3. Beat in egg yolks until mixture becomes creamy.
4. In a large bowl add sugar and pour chocolate mixture over it. Mix well.
5. Add vanilla and continue beating until mixture becomes creamy and spreadable.
6. If icing is too thick, thin with coffee; if too thin, thicken with additional powdered sugar.
7. Ice cake and spread almonds on top before icing hardens.

Chapter 10

# The Sumptuous Sunday Brunch for 20

H-M-M-M . . . SUNDAYS . . . LAZY and wonderful . . . truly blissful. Hours of coffee sipping and newspaper reading followed by that wonderful feeling of laziness and a terrific appetite. It's the perfect time for what is often considered to be one of the most civilized customs of modern man: the leisurely lovely, delicately decadent, sumptuous Sunday brunch. Being two of the biggest fans of this custom, Russell and I consider ourselves experts in the field. We think the following menu is a show-stopper. Designed to please everyone's whim, it is the classic Jewish-Italian Sunday extravaganza.

## THE SUMPTUOUS SUNDAY BRUNCH FOR 20

# *Menu*

**APPETIZER**

*Baked Stuffed Grapefruit*

**ENTRÉE**

*Rolled Soufflé with Cheddar Sauce*

**ACCOMPANIMENTS**

*Sausage Hash Potato Cups*
*Toasted Bagels*

**SALAD**

*Smoked Salmon Salad*

*Bloody Marys (of course)*
*Mimosas*
*Tequila Sunrises*

# *Complete Grocery List*

**Produce:** 10 baking potatoes, or 20 new potatoes
3 bunches fresh parsley
1 bunch fresh dill
10 lemons
4 limes
3 oranges
1 large head red cabbage
2 bunches watercress

2 pounds mushrooms
3 shallots
10 large thin-skinned grapefruit
2 1-pound packages fresh cranberries
1½ pounds pecan pieces
2 pints ripe strawberries
2 heads iceberg lettuce

**Dry Goods:** vegetable oil
salt
paprika
rice or wine vinegar
sugar
catsup
Dijon mustard
fresh pepper
1 large can peeled tomatoes
sweet basil
white pepper

1 small bag flour
1 small jar honey
cinnamon
Worcestershire sauce
Tabasco sauce
celery salt
honey butter
3 jars assorted jams and preserves
2 dozen assorted fresh bagels (or frozen)

**Meat and Fish:** 3 pounds breakfast fresh pork sausage

2 pounds Nova Scotia smoked salmon

**Frozen:** 2 packages chopped spinach

**Dairy:** 3 dozen eggs
1½ pounds butter
1½ pounds grated Parmesan cheese

1 gallon milk
2 8-ounce packages cream cheese
1 pound sharp Cheddar cheese

**Liquor:** 1 quart tequila
4 bottles champagne
2 quarts vodka
1 small bottle grenadine
1 bottle port wine

2 gallons orange juice
2 large cans tomato juice (Sacramento is best!)
mixers

*Paper and* 50 plastic cups
  *Plastic* 50 small paper plates
  *Goods:* 50 large paper plates

50 plastic knives, forks, spoons
50 napkins

  *Addi-* heavy wax paper
  *tional:* 1 jelly-roll pan or cookie sheet with
       edges

## Party Plans

### Day of the Party

Our sumptuous brunch is scheduled for 2:00 P.M. on Sunday.

**Friday**

a. Shop for Complete Grocery List.
b. Prepare 2 Rolled Soufflés with filling (pages 140–141).

**Saturday**

a. Prepare Sausage Hash Potato Cups (see recipe, page 142).
b. Prepare Baked Stuffed Grapefruit up through step 4 (see page 140). Refrigerate tightly covered.
c. Prepare Bloody Mary mix.

**Sunday**

9:00 A.M.   Prepare Cheddar Sauce (see page 142).

10:00 A.M.   Prepare Smoked Salmon Salad. (see recipe, page 143).

11:00 A.M.   Prepare topping for Baked Grapefruit and complete recipe except for baking.

NOON   Set up serving table. Set up bar. Prepare drinks (see recipe, pages 143–144).

1:00 P.M.   a. Split bagels and butter lightly. Set aside.
b. Remove soufflé and potatoes from refrigerator to bring to room temperature.
c. Go get dressed!

1:30 P.M.   a. Place jams and jellies in small bowls with spoons. Set aside.
b. Place cream cheese on small plates. Refrigerate.
c. Preheat oven to 400°.

2:00 P.M.   a. Greet guests. Have them help themselves to the bar.
b. Put grapefruit in preheated oven (last step in recipe) for 15 minutes and serve.
c. When grapefruit is served, pop potatoes and soufflé in 350° oven to heat for 15–20 minutes.
d. Clean grapefruit.
e. Take potatoes from oven and place on serving table. Switch on broiler.
f. Take soufflé from oven, place on serving tray, and cut into 1-inch slices. Place on serving table.
g. Place bagels in broiler. Watch carefully. When golden, remove and place on serving table.
h. Place smoked salmon salad on serving table.
i. Get yourself a drink.
j. Go enjoy your brunch!

# Recipes

## Baked Stuffed Grapefruit

*Yield: 20 grapefruit halves*

INGREDIENTS:

10 large thin-skinned grapefruit
2 1-pound packages fresh cranberries
1½ pounds pecan pieces
1 cup honey
½ cup vodka (optional)
1 teaspoon cinnamon
12 egg whites
½ teaspoon salt
¼ cup sugar
20 ripe strawberries (for garnish)

1. Preheat oven to 400°.
2. Cut grapefruit in half. Core and cut sections, being careful to leave grapefruit intact.
3. In large bowl, combine all ingredients except egg whites, salt, sugar, and strawberries.
4. With electric mixer, beat egg whites with salt till almost stiff.
5. Take cranberry mixture and stuff into core of grapefruit shell, forming small mounds on top.
6. Spread (or pipe with pastry tube) egg whites on top of each grapefruit.
7. Arrange upright on baking sheet, making sure grapefruit is spaced for even browning.
8. Place one ripe strawberry on each one as garnish and bake for 15 minutes or until meringue is golden brown.

## Rolled Soufflé with Cheddar Sauce

*Yield: 15 slices per soufflé*

(Recipe is for one rolled souffle: you will need two rolls.)

*Soufflé*

INGREDIENTS:

½ stick (4 tablespoons) butter
½ cup flour
2 cups scalded milk
8 eggs, separated
1 tablespoon lemon juice
½ cup grated Parmesan cheese
½ teaspoon white pepper
½ teaspoon salt
½ cup finely chopped parsley

1. Preheat oven to 375°.
2. Melt butter over moderate (medium) heat in large saucepan. Add flour gradually, stirring in with whisk. Continue to stir over heat till light golden in color.
3. Slowly pour in milk, whisking while you pour. *Remove from heat.*

4. Add egg yolks one at a time, continuing to whisk till slightly cooled. Set aside.
5. Beat egg whites with salt until stiff peaks form.
6. Add lemon juice, salt, pepper, and grated cheese to cooled mixture.
7. Gently fold in egg whites to mixture.
8. Pour into jelly-roll pans lined with heavy wax paper, greased well.
9. Bake for 20 minutes or until top becomes golden. While soufflé is baking, prepare filling. See recipe below.
10. While soufflé is fairly hot, sprinkle chopped parsley over top.
11. Invert pan onto sheet of waxed paper that is longer than soufflé. Remove the pan lining sheet which is now on top.
12. Spread one-half of filling mixture onto soufflé, saving half for other roll.
13. With aid of waxed paper, carefully roll soufflé from long end. Trim ends and store on cookie sheet. Refrigerate.

### Filling (for 2 soufflé rolls)

INGREDIENTS:

½ stick (¼ pound) butter
2 pounds sliced mushrooms
¼ cup minced shallots
1 large can peeled tomatoes
2 packages frozen chopped spinach
¾ cup grated Parmesan cheese
2 tablespoons sweet basil
1 teaspoon white pepper
1 teaspoon salt

1. Sauté sliced mushrooms and shallots with butter.
2. Drain tomatoes and squeeze dry with hands breaking tomatoes into small pieces. Place in pan with mushrooms and shallots.
3. Thaw and squeeze dry spinach, add to mushroom mixture.
4. On medium heat cook mixture uncovered to remove excess moisture. Remove from heat. Let cool.

*Cheddar Sauce*

INGREDIENTS:

½ cup butter
½ cup flour
2–3 cups milk
2 cups sharp Cheddar cheese
½ cup port wine
½ teaspoon white pepper

1. Melt butter in heavy saucepan.
2. Add flour and whisk until mixture turns light golden.
3. Slowly pour 1 cup milk into mixture, stirring constantly.
4. Add shredded cheese to mixture, letting cheese melt.
5. Add wine and pepper, which will thin sauce.
6. In consistency is a bit thick, add additional milk until desired consistency is reached.

## Sausage Hash Potato Cups

INGREDIENTS:

10 baking potatoes, or 20 new potatoes
3 pounds breakfast fresh pork sausage
1 cup fresh finely chopped parsley
1 teaspoon salt
½ cup vegetable oil
2 teaspoons paprika

1. Preheat oven to 375°.
2. Leaving skins on potatoes, cut in half.
3. With melon baller, scoop out potato, leaving ¼ inch to ½ inch thick shell. Reserve both potato shell and scoopings.
4. Chop or grate potato scoopings.
5. Combine sausage and potato scoopings with salt and chopped parsley.
6. Rub potato shell skins with vegetable oil.
7. Stuff mixture into shells. Sprinkle with paprika.
8. Bake for 45 minutes.

## Smoked Salmon Salad

INGREDIENTS:

2 pounds Nova Scotia smoked salmon
4 cups red cabbage (1 large head)
2 heads iceberg lettuce
2 bunches watercress
1 bunch fresh dill
½ cup rice or wine vinegar
¼ cup sugar
2 tablespoons catsup
1 egg
1 teaspoon freshly grated pepper
  juice of 1 lemon or lime
½ teaspoon salt
3 tablespoons Dijon mustard
1½ cups vegetable oil

1. Cut salmon into small strips. Set aside.
2. Shred cabbage and lettuce.
3. Chop watercress.
4. Remove stems from dill and finely chop.
5. In bowl, add vinegar, sugar, catsup, egg, salt, juice of lemon *or* lime, pepper, and mustard. Mix.
6. With whisk, stir in oil until mixture becomes creamy.
7. Add dill.
8. Toss all ingredients into large bowl. Refrigerate.

## Mimosa

1 part champagne
1 part orange juice
  strawberries for garnish

Combine. Garnish with fresh strawberries.

## Tequila Sunrise

2 parts orange juice
1 part tequila
1 tablespoon grenadine

Mix orange juice and tequila, top with grenadine. Do not stir.

## *Bloody Mary Mix (Quart)*

1 quart tomato juice
¼ cup Worcestershire sauce
½ cup lemon juice
1 teaspoon celery salt
½ teaspoon salt
½ teaspoon Tabasco
½ teaspoon sugar
Freshly ground pepper to taste

Garnish: wedge of lime and stalk of celery.

1. Mix 1 pint vodka to 2 parts Bloody Mary mix.
2. Stir and garnish.

# Chapter 11

# A Perfect Last-Minute Affair for 35

HERE IT IS—the party you can put together in a flash and absolutely enjoy. The time schedule is set for only two days to serve thirty-five people! If you have a wok, pull it out, because we use it here as part of the party visuals on the serving table. The entire meal can be made with or without one, and the fare is sure to be beautiful and delicious. This menu was created for Lord Montague for a party held by the British Tourist Authority in New York City, December 1979.

## A PERFECT LAST-MINUTE AFFAIR FOR 35

# *Menu*

**APPETIZER**

*Cheese Board and Bread Basket*

**ENTRÉE**

*Cashew Chicken and Broccoli in Oyster Sauce
Herbed Rice*

**SALAD**

*Caesar Salad*

**DESSERT**

*Raspberry Mousse with Fresh Strawberries*

*White Wine*

# Complete Grocery List

**Produce:**
- 7 heads broccoli
- 2 pounds raw cashews
- 3 pounds mushrooms
- 2 bunches spring onions (scallions)
- 2 pounds fresh or frozen snowpeas
- 5 lemons
- 1 garlic bulb
- 6 large heads romaine lettuce
- 9 pints fresh strawberries

**Dry Goods:**
- 2 small bottles oyster sauce
- garlic powder
- Worcestershire sauce
- 1 bottle teriyaki sauce
- sesame oil
- 4 pounds long grain rice
- 2 13-ounce cans chicken stock
- sweet basil
- dill
- tarragon
- white pepper
- salt
- parsley flakes
- bay leaves
- Dijon mustard
- 1 can anchovies in oil
- rice or wine vinegar
- olive oil
- safflower oil
- 1 package croutons (unless homemade are used)
- 1 small box gelatin
- 1 box superfine sugar
- 1 large can Sterno
- 7 loaves fresh assorted breads

**Poultry:**
- 12 pounds boneless breast of chicken

**Frozen:**
- 8 packages frozen raspberries

**Dairy:**
- 1 pound Cheddar cheese
- 1 pound Brie
- 1 pound Jarlsberg cheese
- 1 pound Muenster
- 1 pound Boursin
- 1 pound butter
- 2½ pints heavy cream
- ½ pint sour cream
- ½ pound grated Parmesan cheese (packaged in two equal halves)
- 2 dozen eggs

**Liquor:**
- 2 cases dry white wine
- 6 quarts mineral water

*Paper*
*Goods:* 40 dinner size paper plates      tablecloth
100 plastic cups      40 dessert plates
40 forks and/or pairs of chopsticks      40 spoons
50 dinner napkins

*Equip-*
*ment:* 1 cheese board
bread baskets
1 large salad bowl
1 large serving bowl for mousse
1 large platter

Party time is 8:00 P.M.

**Day before Party**

a. Grocery shop for all ingredients.
b  Cut up and marinate chicken (see recipe on page 152).
c. Make Raspberry Mousse (see recipe on pages 154–155).

## Party Plans

| | | |
|---|---|---|
| ***Day of the*** | MORNING | Chill wine. |
| ***Party*** | NOON | Prepare Caesar Salad (see page 154). |
| | 1:30 P.M. | Prepare Herbed Rice (see page 153). |
| | 2:30 P.M. | Prepare Cashew Chicken and Broccoli in Oyster Sauce (see recipe, pages 152–153). |
| | 4:30 P.M. | Tidy up kitchen. |
| | 5:30 P.M. | Set up buffet table with wok in center of table over Sterno container. |
| | 6:00 P.M. | Whip garnish cream for Raspberry Mousse (see recipe, page 155). |
| | 6:30 P.M. | Set up Cheese Board and Bread Basket (see page 152). |
| | 7:00 P.M. | Get dressed. |

8:00 P.M.
a. Greet guests.
b. Pop Cashew Chicken and Broccoli into 350° oven for 20 minutes.
c. Punch holes in aluminum foil cover of rice and put into oven with chicken.
d. While chicken and rice are heating, toss salad with dressing and extra cheese in bag, saving one-third of the croutons for top of salad.
e. Fill salad bowl, top with croutons. Place on table. Bring wok to kitchen.
f. Take chicken from oven and place in wok. Put on table over Sterno (which has been lighted).
g. Place warmed rice in bowl and place on table.
h. Go have fun!
i. When dinner is cleared, garnish mousse with whipped cream, place mousse bowl in center of large platter with stawberries around it. Place on serving table.

# Recipes

## Cheese Board and Bread Basket

*Cheeses*

1 pound Cheddar
1 pound Brie
1 pound Jarlsberg
1 pound Muenster
1 pound Boursin

*Breads*

7 loaves: an assortment of dark and light breads, the freshest possible.

## Cashew Chicken with Broccoli in Oyster Sauce

INGREDIENTS:

7 heads broccoli
12 pounds boneless breast of chicken
1 large bottle teriyaki sauce
12 tablespoons (1 stick) butter for chicken*
2 tablespoons garlic powder
2 lemons, juiced
3 tablespoons Worcestershire sauce
2 tablespoons sesame oil
2 bunches spring onions, minced
6 tablespoons butter for mushrooms
3 pounds sliced mushrooms
2 small bottles oyster sauce
2 pounds cleaned, destemmed snowpeas
2 pounds raw cashews

1. Cut stems off broccoli, separating flowerets into bite-size pieces.
2. Cut chicken breasts into small bite-size strips (about 1½-inch by 1½-inch). Put in bowl and pour bottle of teriyaki sauce over it. Mix well. Marinate overnight in refrigerator.
3. In wok or large skillet, heat 2 tablespoons butter (or butter and oil) until it bubbles.
4. Add enough chicken pieces to cover bottom. Stir-fry.
5. Sprinkle each batch of chicken with garlic powder, lemon juice, Worcestershire sauce, and sesame oil.
6. Stir-fry until chicken is white and cooked. Remove to aluminum baking pan and repeat with next batch. (It should take about six batches).
7. Stir-fry spring onions and mushrooms in three batches. Heat 2 tablespoons butter each time. Sauté mushrooms till tender. Sprinkle each batch with lemon juice.
8. Put cooked spring onions and mushrooms in pan with chicken. Empty in 1 bottle of oyster sauce. Mix well.
9. Blanch broccoli in salted boiling water for one minute. Rinse with cold water. Drain thoroughly.

10. Add broccoli to chicken and mushrooms.
11. If snowpeas are frozen, thaw and do not cook. If fresh, blanch same as broccoli. Add to pan.
12. Add cashews and second bottle of oyster sauce. Toss.
13. Cover with foil, set aside.

   * If using a wok, substitute ½ cup oil for ½ cup butter.

## Herbed Rice

INGREDIENTS:

7 cups long grain rice
2 13-ounce cans chicken stock
10 cups water
½ stick butter
1 tablespoon sweet basil
2 cloves garlic, pressed
2 teaspoons dill
½ teaspoon tarragon
1 teaspoon white pepper
1 tablespoon Worcestershire sauce
2 teaspoons salt
4 tablespoons parsley flakes
2 large bay leaves

1. Place all ingredients into 8-quart saucepan with tight-fitting lid, or divide ingredients and cook in two batches.
2. Bring to boil. Simmer covered 17 minutes, stirring occasionally.
3. Remove from heat and empty into baking pan to cool.
4. When cooled, cover with aluminum foil.

## Caesar Salad

INGREDIENTS:

6 large heads romaine
2 teaspoons Dijon mustard
1 can anchovies in oil
2 cloves garlic
1 teaspoon white pepper
½ cup rice or wine vinegar
2 tablespoons Worcestershire sauce
2 lemons, juiced
2 eggs
½ cup olive oil
1 cup safflower oil
½ pound fresh grated Parmesan cheese, divided in half
1 box croutons, or homemade

1. Clean romaine and break into bite-size pieces. Dry thoroughly, or spin, and place in very large salad bowl or plastic bag. (If you fit the bag into a cardboard box it will be easier to fill.) Refrigerate in bag.
2. In blender combine the other ingredients except olive and safflower oil, croutons, and ¼ pound Parmesan cheese. Blend at high speed for 5 seconds.
3. Turn motor off and add oil. Blend an additional 5 seconds. Empty into large jar or container. Refrigerate.
4. Hold aside croutons and ¼ pound cheese for sprinkling on top of salad when tossed.

## Raspberry Mousse with Fresh Strawberries

*Mousse*

INGREDIENTS:

8 packages frozen raspberries
2 tablespoons lemon juice
1 cup superfine sugar
2 packages gelatin
12 eggs, separated
½ pint sour cream
1½ pints heavy cream
½ teaspoon salt

*Garnish*

INGREDIENTS:

1 pint heavy cream
½ cup superfine sugar
9 pints fresh strawberries

1. Thaw raspberries and drain for juice. Reserve liquid.
2. Put raspberries through food mill or sieve to remove seeds.
3. Place raspberry juice in small saucepan with lemon juice. Warm on medium heat.

4. Add cup of superfine sugar, stirring to dissolve.
5. Put gelatin in blender, add juice, and blend at high speed for 5 seconds.
6. Place egg yolks and sour cream in blender with juice mixture. Blend 5 seconds at high speed.
7. Combine blender ingredients and raspberries in large bowl.
8. Whip 1½ pints heavy cream till stiff and fold into raspberry mixture.
9. Beat egg whites with salt until soft peaks form; fold gently into raspberry mixture.
10. Refrigerate in large serving bowl.
11. Just before serving, prepare garnish by whipping 1 pint heavy cream and ½ cup sugar together. Refrigerate separately.
12. Brush any dirt off strawberries, destem, and refrigerate separately.
13. Before serving, garnish top with whipped cream piped on with pastry tube, if possible. Strawberries are placed around the bowl on plate underneath for visual effect.

# Chapter 12

# A Kiddie Party for 15

THERE IS NO party more fun to cater than this one. The menu is created with kiddie tastes in mind and serves fifteen children. Each child is served his own personalized box or bag with the first four menu items in it. Shoe boxes, mushroom baskets, or even brown paper lunch bags can be made festive with paper, paints, and ribbons, with each child's name on his or hers. The meal is topped with a create-your-own-sundae smorgasbord and fascinating Party Cone Cakes! Our Party Plan schedule is designed for a Saturday afternoon.

## A KIDDIE PARTY FOR 15

# *Menu*

**ENTRÉE**

*Barbecued Chicken*

**ACCOMPANIMENT**

*Potato Chip Curls*
*Fresh Fruit*

**DESSERT**

*A Bag of Nuts and Raisins with Prize*
*Party Cone Cakes*
*Ice Cream Smorgasbord*

*Pink Party Punch*

# Complete Grocery List

**Produce:**
1 large onion
garlic bulb
15 to 20 medium-size round
   potatoes

1 bag chopped nuts
2 large boxes raisins
4 large cans mixed party nuts
15 pieces fresh seasonal fruit

**Dry Goods:**
2 16-ounce cans tomato sauce
1 small jar Dijon mustard
1 quart vegetable oil
1 box brown sugar
rice vinegar
Worcestershire sauce
Tabasco sauce
salt
white pepper
1 pound sugar
1 box cake flour

cream of tartar
1 small can or box of cocoa
2 dozen flat-bottom ice cream cones
2 cans prepared white frosting
1 small container chocolate sprinkles
2 jars chocolate topping
2 jars marshmallow topping
2 jars strawberry topping
2 jars caramel topping
1 jar cherries

NOTE: If you are interested in a natural, more healthy Ice Cream Smorgasbord, select a variety of toppings such as coconut, wheat germ, honey and fresh fruit.

**Poultry:**
8 pounds or 30 pieces chicken,
   thighs and legs

**Frozen:**
1 can frozen lime juice concentrate

**Dairy:**
4 half-gallons assorted ice cream
   flavors
1 dozen eggs
1½ pints heavy cream

**Beverages:**
4 quarts cranberry juice
3 quarts ginger ale
1 quart club soda
1 5-pound block ice

| *Special* | punch bowl |
| *Equip-* | German radish curler |
| *ment:* | 15 little prizes |

| *Paper* | 15 decorated party bags or boxes | 45 plastic cups |
| *Goods:* | 1 box plastic sandwich bags | 15 plastic spoons |
| | 50 dinner napkins | 2 dozen bowls for ice cream |

## Party Plans

### Wednesday

a. Shop for all ingredients except chicken and fruit, and possibly ice cream if freezer space is a problem.

b. Make barbecue sauce for chicken (see recipe, page 164). Store in container, tightly covered, in refrigerator.

### Thursday

a. Bake Party Cone Cakes (see recipe, page 165), frost, and store on cookie sheet in refrigerator.

b. Make up the baskets, bags, or boxes for each child.

### Friday

a. Pick up fruit and chicken. Prepare chicken, store in baggies in refrigerator.

b. Prepare Potato Chip Curls (see recipe on pages 164–165). Store in sandwich bags. No need to refrigerate.

## Day of the Party

### Saturday

MORNING

a. Package raisins and party nuts together with prize in a sandwich bag for each child.

b. Set up table for punch and paper goods.

c. Pick up 5-pound block ice.

NOON    Pack each child's basket with 2 pieces of chicken, raisin and nut mixture, Party Potato Curls, and a piece of fresh fruit.

12:30 P.M.    Make the punch.

1:00 P.M.    Greet your little guests with their own basket!

3:00 P.M.    Clear away the remains of lunch. Put out the Ice Cream Smorgasbord and Party Cone Cakes.

*Have fun watching . . . we do!*

# Recipes

## Barbecued Chicken

*Barbecue Sauce*

INGREDIENTS:

2 8-ounce cans tomato sauce
1 large onion, finely minced
½ cup vegetable oil
¾ cup rice vinegar
⅓ cup brown sugar
1 large clove garlic, peeled and finely minced
3 tablespoons Dijon mustard
2 tablespoons Worcestershire sauce
¼ teaspoon Tabasco sauce
½ teaspoon salt
¼ teaspoon white pepper
½ can frozen concentrate (undiluted) lime juice

1. Sauté onion in oil in large saucepan until transparent.
2. Add vinegar and brown sugar, stirring until bubbly.
3. Add rest of ingredients. Simmer 15 minutes over low heat. Then turn off and let cool. Store in container, covered tightly, and refrigerate.

*Chicken*

8 pounds chicken thighs and legs (1 leg and 1 thigh each serving)

1. Preheat oven to 350°.
2. Arrange chicken legs and thighs in large baking pan.
3. Pour 2 cups of sauce over chicken. Cover with aluminum foil.
4. Bake for ½ hour.
5. Remove from oven, drain. Spread out chicken pieces on cookie sheet.
6. Brush on additional sauce. Broil until sauce begins to dot black on chicken.
7. Remove, cool, and place each piece individually in a plastic sandwich bag. Refrigerate.

## Potato Chip Curls*

INGREDIENTS:

15–20 medium-size round potatoes, well scrubbed
1 quart oil for deep frying
salt to taste

1. Holding potato at bottom, stick screw in top of potato, and with a clockwise motion, spiral down each potato with radish curler.
2. Heat oil in large skillet, wok, or deep fryer.
3. Cook potato chip curls two at a time in hot oil.

4. Remove and drain on paper towels and sprinkle with salt while hot.
5. Cool and place individually in plastic sandwich bags.

\* See illustration.

## Party Cone Cakes!

INGREDIENTS:

  12 eggs, separated
   2 cups sugar
   2 cups sifted cake flour
  ¾ cup cocoa
  ½ cup cold water
  ½ teaspoon cream of tartar
  ¾ teaspoon salt
   2 dozen flat-bottom ice cream cones
   2 cans prepared white frosting
     chocolate sprinkles

1. Preheat oven to 375°.
2. Beat egg yolks till thick (about 5 minutes) with electric mixer.
3. Beat sugar in gradually.
4. Beat in flour and cocoa, alternating with cold water. Set aside.
5. In large bowl, beat egg whites, cream of tartar, and salt with electric beater at high speed, until stiff.
6. Gradually and gently fold the egg yolk mixture into the stiff egg whites.
7. Pour batter into cones. Fill two-thirds full.
8. Bake standing up on cookie sheet for 20 minutes, or until cake springs back when touched.
9. When cool, ice with frosting and top with sprinkles.

## Ice Cream Smorgasbord

INGREDIENTS:*

4 half-gallon containers of assorted ice cream
2 jars chocolate topping
2 jars marshmallow topping
2 jars strawberry topping
2 jars caramel
1 jar cherries
1½ pints heavy cream, whipped

1. At dessert time, place ice cream in four large bowls, place toppings, cherries, and whipped cream in individual bowls with serving spoons.
2. Arrange on table with dessert bowls and spoons.
3. Stand back and watch the fun!

* There is another way of doing this—a more natural, healthy smorgasbord, if you prefer it. In that case, select healthy toppings such as raisins, fresh coconut, toasted wheat germ, fresh fruit, and honey.

## Pink Party Punch

INGREDIENTS:

4 quarts cranberry juice
3 quarts ginger ale
1 quart club soda
1 5-pound block ice

Combine all ingredients in punch bowl with ice.

Chapter 13

# The Grand Affair for over 100: Your Daughter's Wedding or Your Son's Bar Mitzvah!

TO CELEBRATE THE most beautiful special events in life . . . the "grand affair" arises. Occasions like your "little girl" getting married, or your "baby boy" getting bar mitzvahed are so very special that they deserve the best of festivities, but the cost of these events has been known to put people in debt for years.

Well . . . it no longer has to be that way. You can cater your own elegant affair very reasonably and most beautifully.

The project, of course, is a large one, but very often friends can be enlisted and the preparation can be its own party as you work together for a very special cause.

On the next pages you will learn how to handle an affair on a grand scale. Over a hundred guests will gather to enjoy a fabulous party—*your* party—and even the chefs will have time to enjoy!

## Planning Your Party

There is a definite choice to be made early on as to the type of affair you would like to cater, depending on preference and budget.

The first type of affair uses paper and plastic products. This cuts the cost of the event dramatically, and in terms of staff, only one bartender and four helpers for cleanup are necessary.

The second type of affair involves the rental of glass and china goods. Staffing then becomes more important as two bartenders and six helpers in service and cleanup are necessary. If you do intend to use rentals and additional staff, be sure to read over chapter 14 several times.

*The Grand Affair for over 100*

# *Menu*

### HORS D'OEUVRES

*Caviar Mousse*
*Stuffed Mushrooms with Herbed Cheese*
*Zucchini Cups with Seviche*
*Bread, Fruit, and Cheese Board*

### BUFFET

*King of Hearts Salad*
*Chicken Breasts with Mushroom Dijon Sauce*
*Smoked Ham, Turkey, or Fish*
*with Creamy Cognac Horseradish Dressing*
*Garden Goddess Salad*
*Mixed Greens with Salad Supreme Dressing*
*Herbed Rice Vinaigrette*

### DESSERT

*Wedding or Bar Mitzvah Cake\**

*Champagne Punch*
*Full Bar*

\* Cake is ordered from your favorite bakery or is the special and separate project of the baker in the family!

# Full Grocery List

NOTE: Space in a refrigerator will be of the utmost importance. If you have limited space, check around for "borrowed" space with friends, or rent a refrigerator for the week before the party.

**Produce:**
½ pound shallots
3 bulbs garlic
14 bunches parsley
30 medium-size zucchini
12 limes
2 large red peppers
1 bunch fresh dill (if unavailable, dried)
11 pounds medium-size mushrooms
24 lemons
5 pounds green beans
6 large Bermuda onions

5 bunches or pounds fresh asparagus
6 small, or 4 large heads cauliflower
8 heads broccoli
4 pounds white turnips
4 pounds carrots
4 bunches scallions
6 bunches red radishes
6 bunches watercress
10 heads Boston lettuce
5 heads romaine lettuce
6 Belgian endives

**Dry Goods:**
1 large bottle lemon juice or 2 dozen lemons to fresh squeeze
1 small package gelatin
3 quarts or 18 cans chicken stock
1 small jar mayonnaise
white pepper
1 jar chives
Tabasco sauce
Worcestershire sauce
10 cans artichoke hearts
5 cans hearts of palm
1 can anchovies
4 quarts peanut oil
sweet basil
bay leaves

tarragon
2 1-quart bottles rice vinegar
1 16-ounce jar pimentos
½ pound roasted sesame seeds
2 quarts vegetable oil (unprocessed, unrefined if possible)
2 8-ounce jars Dijon mustard
1 bottle soy sauce or tamari
2 jars white horseradish
salt
12 pounds long grain white rice
oregano
1 tube anchovy paste
1 dozen loaves assorted breads
1-pound box superfine sugar

**Meat, Poultry, Fish:**
4 ounces red lumpfish caviar
20 pounds top butt sirloin (thick and lean)
30 pounds boneless chicken breasts

30 pounds smoked ham *or* turkey *or* fish (boneless)
5 pounds flounder or sole

*Frozen:* 2 packages corn kernels

*Dairy:* 1½ dozen eggs      2¼ pounds butter
7 8-ounce packages cream cheese      3 quarts, 1 pint sour cream
1 4-ounce package cream cheese      2 quarts buttermilk
2 pints heavy cream      1 large wheel Brie cheese
6 packages Alouette herb cheese      1 4-pound wedge Jarlsberg cheese
1 pound ricotta cheese      1 3-pound wedge Cheddar cheese
2 pounds fresh grated Parmesan

*Cooking Liquor:* 2 fifths white wine
1 pint bottle cognac

*Full Bar:* 2 quarts brandy      1 quart Canadian Club
8 quarts vodka      2 quarts Cointreau
3 quarts gin      3 cases white wine
4 quarts Scotch      1 case champagne
1 quart bourbon      80 pounds ice cubes and 2 5-pound
1 quart rum          blocks of ice
1 quart tequila

*Mixers:* 12 quarts tonic      2 6-packs Tab
12 quarts club soda      1 case mineral water
6 quarts ginger ale      1½ gallons orange juice
6 quarts Coke

*Extras:* plastic wrap      empty cardboard boxes
aluminum foil      several rolls paper towels
large plastic bags      flowers

*If using paper service:*

*Paper Goods:* 400 plastic 10-ounce glasses      150 plastic knives
200 heavy paper or plastic dinner      300 dinner napkins
     plates      300 cocktail napkins
150 dessert plates
300 plastic forks

*If using rentals:*

*Equipment:* 300 10-ounce all-purpose stemware      125 napkins (linen)
150 dinner plates      linen tableclothes*
250 forks      salt and pepper shakers (2 per table)
125 cups and saucers      2 large punch bowls (1 for fruit, 1 for
125 dessert plates          punch)
125 small dessert bowls      1 4-quart chafing dish for chicken
3 sets creamers and sugar bowls          with 1 extra insert
2 dozen ashtrays      4 large platters
2 100-cup coffee urns      3 large salad bowls

* The rental of tables and chairs must be done according to space. Ideally, 13 round tables would be rented, each able to sit 10, and a buffet table for the fruit and cheese. Linens would be ordered accordingly.

## Party Plans

Our affair is planned for a Saturday afternoon at 4:00 P.M. As always, the time schedule can be easily adjusted if necessary.

**In advance**

a. Entertainment should be arranged for one month ahead if desired.
b. Cake should be ordered or arranged for one month before the party.
c. If using rentals, they should be ordered two weeks before party for Friday (day before) delivery.
d. Staff should be arranged for two weeks before party.

## The Week of the Party

**Monday**

a. Order ice and liquor and have delivered Saturday of party.
b. Purchase bar mixers and paper goods.
c. Order smoked meat and have sliced by butcher.
d. Order flowers for tables and extras for garnishing platters.

**Tuesday**

Shop for Seviche and Caviar Mousse ingredients.

GROCERY LIST

| | |
|---|---|
| 1 lemon | 1 bunch fresh parsley |
| 1 small package gelatin | white pepper |
| 1 can chicken stock | 12 limes |
| 2 shallots, or 1 small onion | 5 pounds flounder or sole |
| 3 eggs | or any thin, delicate fish |
| 4 ounces red lumpfish caviar | 1 bunch fresh dill or jar of dried |
| 1 jar mayonnaise | 2 packages frozen corn kernels |
| 1 4-ounce package cream cheese | 2 large red peppers |
| 1 bulb garlic | 1 jar chives |
| ½ pint heavy cream | Tabasco sauce |

**Wednesday**

a. Prepare Seviche only (see recipe, page 179), Zucchini Caps will be prepared later in the week.
b. Prepare Caviar Mousse (see recipe, page 178).
c. Shop for ingredients of Chicken Breasts with Mushroom Dijon Sauce, Salad Supreme Dressing, Creamy Cognac Horseradish Dressing.

GROCERY LIST

| | |
|---|---|
| 30 pounds boneless chicken breasts | 2 bottles white wine |
| 6 pounds fresh mushrooms | 2 pounds butter |
| | 1 cup Dijon mustard (8-ounce jar) |

1 bulb fresh garlic
1 small bottle soy sauce or
  tamari
2 quarts, 1 pint sour cream
salt
1 quart peanut oil
1 quart buttermilk
4 eggs
5 lemons
oregano

Worcestershire sauce
1 tube or small can
  anchovy paste
6 bunches parsley
2 jars white horseradish
4 8-ounce packages cream
  cheese
1 pint heavy cream
1 small bottle cognac
2 quarts rice vinegar

## Thursday

a. Prepare Chicken Breast with Mushroom Dijon Sauce (see recipes, page 181).
b. Prepare Salad Supreme Dressing (see recipe, page 183).
c. Prepare Creamy Cognac Horseradish Dressing (see page 181).
d. Shop for all other ingredients, except smoked meat and breads.

GROCERY LIST

20 pounds top butt sirloin
  (thick and lean)
5 pounds green beans
10 cans artichoke hearts
5 cans hearts of palm
6 large Bermuda onions
1 bulb garlic
1 can anchovies
7 bunches parsley
3 quarts peanut oil
2 pounds fresh grated
  Parmesan
10 lemons
8 eggs
½ pound hulled, roasted
  sesame seeds
1 6-ounce jar pimentos
5 bunches or pounds thin
  asparagus
6 small, or 4 large heads
  cauliflower
8 heads broccoli
4 pounds white turnips
4 pounds carrots
4 bunches scallions
6 bunches radishes
6 bunches watercress
1 quart buttermilk
1 quart sour cream

1 pint rice vinegar
1 small jar Dijon Mustard
10 heads Boston lettuce
5 heads romaine lettuce
6 Belgian endives
10 pounds long grain
  white rice
2 quarts vegetable oil
½ pound shallots
bay leaves
tarragon
1 large wheel Brie
1 4-pound wedge Jarlsberg
1 3-pound wedge Cheddar
5 pounds medium-size
  mushrooms
6 packages Alouette herb
  cheese
3 8-ounce packages cream
  cheese
1 pound ricotta cheese
30 medium-size zucchini
1½ gallons orange juice
plastic wrap
several rolls paper towels
aluminum foil
large plastic bags
2 empty cartons
1-pound box superfine sugar

NOTE: If using paper service, check complete grocery list and pick up all items today.

**Friday**

a. Purchase breads (1 dozen assorted loaves).
b. Prepare King of Hearts Salad (page 180), Garden Goddess Salad (page 182), Mixed Greens (page 182), Stuffed Mushrooms (page 179), and Stuffed Zucchini Cups (page 179).
c. Pick up smoked meat.
d. Prepare rice (page 183) and vinaigrette (page 184), but do not toss together till Saturday.

## *Day of the Party*

**Saturday**

8:00 A.M.
a. Set up rentals (if using).
b. Prepare room.
c. Set up bar.

10:00 A.M.  Accept liquor, ice, and flower deliveries.

11:00 A.M.  Arrange fruit and cheese board with breads on buffet table. Accompany with cutting board and bread and cheese knives.

NOON
a. Helpers should arrive.
b. Begin arranging platters of food and cover with plastic wrap. Place appetizer platters and cheese board together and near bar.
c. Keep main course platters in kitchen until 5:00 P.M.

2:00 P.M.
a. Get dressed.
b. Have staff continue arranging platters and completing any details of setup still needed.

2:30 P.M.  Bartenders arrive.

3:00 P.M.  Enjoy the wedding or bar mitzvah.

4:00 P.M.
a. Return to your magnificent reception.
b. Get the bar going.
c. Uncover hors d'oeuvre platters. Preheat oven to 375°.

4:30 P.M.  Bake chicken for ½ hour.

5:00 P.M.  Have the help set up main course, toss rice with vinaigrette, and assist with buffet.

6:00 P.M.
a. Have help clear dinner plates, set up dessert, and cut the cake.
b. This was a big one. Be sure to have a glass of champagne, put your feet up, and relax!

# Recipes

## Cheese Bread Board

1 large wheel Brie
1 4-pound wedge Jarlsberg
1 3-pound wedge Cheddar cheese
   A dozen loaves of assorted breads

## Caviar Mousse

INGREDIENTS:

   1 tablespoon lemon juice
   2 shallots, or 1 small onion
   1 clove garlic
   2 envelopes gelatin
   ⅔ cup hot chicken stock
   3 eggs, separated
   ½ cup mayonnaise
   1 4-ounce package softened cream cheese
   ½ teaspoon white pepper
   2 tablespoons chopped parsley
   1 cup heavy cream
   4 ounces red lumpfish caviar

1. Place lemon juice, shallots, garlic, and gelatin in blender jar.
2. Pour in heated chicken stock.
3. Blend 10 seconds at high speed.
4. Add to blender jar: 3 egg yolks, ½ cup mayonnaise, cream cheese, white pepper and chopped parsley.
5. Blend 20 seconds at high speed, and with motor running pour in heavy cream.
6. Beat egg whites till stiff.
7. In large mixing bowl, fold in caviar with blended ingredients.
8. Then fold in egg white.
9. Pour in 2-quart Jell-O mold and refrigerate.

## Stuffed Mushrooms with Herbed Cheese

*Yield: Approximately 100 mushrooms*

INGREDIENTS:

5 pounds medium-size mushrooms
6 packages Alouette herb cheese
3 8-ounce packages cream cheese
1 pound ricotta cheese
1 bunch parsley, finely chopped
1 lemon, squeezed
1 tablespoon Worcestershire sauce

1. Destem mushrooms and wipe with damp cloth, reserving stems.
2. Combine all other ingredients.
3. Stuff into caps.
4. Chop mushroom stem pieces and sprinkle on top of stuffed mushroom.
5. Place on cookie sheets, wrap well with foil, and refrigerate.

## Zucchini Cups with Seviche

*Yield: Approximately 150 zucchini cups*

### Seviche

INGREDIENTS:

5 pounds flounder or sole, or any thin, delicate fish
12 limes squeezed, reserve liquid
2 packages frozen corn kernels
2 large red peppers, finely chopped
1 jar chives
1 teaspoon Tabasco sauce
1 tablespoon dill

1. Cut fish into very thin, 4-inch-length strips.
2. Pour lime juice over fish.
3. Mix in remaining ingredients.
4. Cover and let sit 4 hours at room temperature, stirring occasionally.
5. Refrigerate tightly covered.

### Zucchini Cups

INGREDIENT:

30 medium-size zucchini

1. Clean and scrub zucchini carefully, removing any traces of sand.
2. Cut into 1-inch sections. Scoop out insides of each section with melon baller, being careful not to pierce bottom. Discard pulp.
3. Stuff cap with Seviche, place on cookie sheet, cover well with foil, and refrigerate.

## King of Hearts Salad

INGREDIENTS:

20 pounds top butt sirloin (thick and lean)
5 pounds green beans, fresh, trimmed if possible, frozen if not
6 large Bermuda onions
6 cloves garlic
4 bunches parsley
1 can anchovies
1 cup lemon juice
3 cups rice vinegar
4 eggs, room temperature
1 tablespoon sweet basil
2 quarts peanut oil
10 cans artichoke hearts
5 cans hearts of palm
1 6-ounce jar pimentos
4 cups fresh grated Parmesan cheese

1. Broil sirloins rare, careful not to overcook. Let cool and refrigerate.
2. Blanch green beans, if fresh, 5 minutes in boiling water. Drain and cool. If frozen, defrost.
3. Peel and chop onions into coarse pieces and set aside.
4. In blender jar, combine 3 garlic cloves, 3 bunches parsley, ½ can anchovies, ½ cup lemon juice, 1½ cups rice vinegar, 2 eggs, and ½ tablespoon basil. Blend on medium-high speed 15 seconds, then reduce speed and drizzle in oil to fill jar.
5. Empty contents into large bowl and repeat process with *same* remaining ingredients. Add any excess oil to ingredients in bowl, stirring till combined.
6. Drain artichoke hearts; cut into quarters. Add to bowl of dressing. Let stand at room temperature.
7. Drain and slice hearts of palm into ½-inch rounds. Also add to dressing in bowl.
8. When steaks have chilled, cut into julienne strips, 1½ to 2 inches long, ¼ inch thick.
9. Cut pimentos into small strips, reserving one-third of the strips for garnish. Add the rest to steak mixture.
10. In a very large container (a cardboard box with a trashcan liner works great) add Parmesan and toss all ingredients and refrigerate.

## Chicken Breasts with Mushroom Dijon Sauce

INGREDIENTS:

30 pounds boneless chicken breasts*
2 pounds butter
6 pounds fresh mushrooms
2 fifths white wine
5 cloves garlic, minced
1 teaspoon salt
1 teaspoon white pepper
4 bunches fresh parsley, chopped fine
1 cup Dijon mustard
2 quarts sour cream
¼ cup soy sauce

1. Cut chicken fillets into 1-inch by 2-inch strips.
2. In a heavy skillet, sauté the chicken fillets in butter over medium-high heat, browning the surface—does *not* have to be cooked through.
3. Place chicken in 2 large roasting pans; set aside. When ready to serve bake 30 minutes in 375° oven.
4. Slice mushrooms with stems left on. In 2 tablespoons butter and ½ cup wine, sauté mushrooms with garlic, salt, and pepper a portion at a time till limp and wet, with a sprinkling of parsley. Add to chicken in roasting pans, dividing evenly.
5. In large saucepan, add remaining butter, wine, as well as mustard. Whisk until smooth, adding sour cream, soy sauce, and any remaining parsley.
6. When mixture has reached creamy consistency, pour over chicken in roasting pans, dividing evenly.
7. Cover tightly with foil after cooling slightly and refrigerate.

* When ordering your chicken, have your butcher skin and pound the breasts into fillets ½ inch thick.

## Smoked Ham, Turkey, or Fish with Creamy Cognac Horseradish Dressing

INGREDIENTS:

4 8-ounce packages cream cheese
2 jars white horseradish
2 lemons
¼ cup cognac
1 pint heavy cream, whipped
1 bunch parsley, minced fine
30 pounds smoked, boneless meat or fish of your choice

1. Let cream cheese come to room temperature unwrapped in large bowl.
2. Drain horseradish; add to cream cheese, blending with fork till creamy.
3. Squeeze lemons and add juice.
4. Add cognac, whipped heavy cream, and parsley.
5. Blend, cover tightly with plastic wrap, and refrigerate.
6. Serve on side of meat or fish.

### Garden Goddess Salad

INGREDIENTS:

4 pounds white turnips
6 small, or 4 large heads cauliflower
8 heads broccoli
5 pounds or bunches fresh asparagus as thin as possible
4 pounds carrots
6 bunches red radishes
4 eggs, room temperature
2 cups rice or wine vinegar
    salt and pepper to taste
½ cup Dijon mustard
4 bunches watercress
1 quart peanut oil
1 quart buttermilk
1 quart sour cream
4 bunches scallions (for garnish)

1. Prepare vegetables by cutting into attractive bite-size pieces.
2. Blanch turnips and cauliflowers in boiling water for approximately 3 to 5 minutes, then plunge into cold water. Let cool and drain.
3. Blanche broccoli and asparagus in boiling water for approximately 2 minutes, then plunge into cold water. Let cool and drain.
4. Toss blanched vegetables together with carrots and radishes. Set aside.
5. In a blender jar, place 2 eggs, 1 cup vinegar, salt, pepper, Dijon mustard, and 1 bunch watercress. Blend at high speed 15 seconds or until watercress becomes pulverized. With motor running, drizzle in 2 cups oil until mixture is a thick consistency. Empty into large mixing bowl. Repeat with second batch and empty into bowl.
6. Place 2 remaining bunches of watercress in a blender jar. Pour in 2 cups buttermilk, pulverize watercress, and add to mixing bowl.
7. Add remaining buttermilk and sour cream to mixing bowl. Stir well.
8. Toss dressing with vegetables in a plastic bag placed in a cardboard carton. Twist tie bag and refrigerate.
9. Garnish with scallions.

### Mixed Greens with Salad Supreme Dressing

*Greens*

INGREDIENTS:

10 heads Boston lettuce
5 heads romaine
2 bunches watercress
6 Belgian endive
½ pound roasted, hulled sesame seeds

### Dressing

INGREDIENTS:

¾ cup rice vinegar
4 eggs, room temperature
¼ cup lemon juice
4 cloves garlic
2 tablespoons basil
1 tablespoon oregano
2 tablespoons Worcestershire sauce
2 tablespoons anchovy paste
1 bunch parsley
2 teaspoons white pepper
2 teaspoons salt
2 cups peanut oil
1 pint sour cream
1 quart buttermilk

1. In blender jar, add all ingredients except peanut oil, sour cream, and buttermilk. Blend on medium high speed 15 seconds.
2. With motor running, drizzle in peanut oil.
3. Empty contents into large mixing bowl. Combine thoroughly with sour cream and buttermilk.
4. Place in container with lid and refrigerate.

### Herbed Rice Vinaigrette

### *Herbed Rice*

(Recipe needs to made *four times!*)

INGREDIENTS:

6 cups long grain white rice
4 shallots, finely minced
2 cloves garlic, peeled, minced
½ stick butter
1 tablespoon basil
2 bay leaves
1 tablespoon Worcestershire sauce
3 cups chicken broth
9 cups water
1 teaspoon pepper
1 teaspoon salt

1. Place all ingredients in 8-quart pot. Bring to boil and simmer, covered, 17 minutes.
2. Remove from heat and transfer to large foil roasting pan. Let cool.
3. Prepare Vinaigrette.

## Vinaigrette

(Only one batch needed for all rice)

INGREDIENTS:

1½ pints rice or wine vinegar
2 quarts vegetable oil (unrefined and unprocessed recommended)
2 bunches parsley, chopped fine
½ cup lemon juice
1 teaspoon salt

1. Place ingredients in mixing bowl and combine thoroughly.
2. Toss with all four batches cooked rice in large roasting pans.

## Champagne Punch

INGREDIENTS:

1 quart vodka
½ quart Cointreau
½ quart brandy
3 bottles champagne
1 bottle club soda
½ cup superfine sugar

1. In large punch bowl mix all ingredients and add 5-pound block of ice.

# Chapter 14

# Planning Large Affairs

FOR A LARGE-SCALE affair, several additional factors come into play in terms of the hiring of helpers and the securing of rentals.

# The Hiring of Service

## Bartender

*Number needed:* One good bartender can easily service fifty people.

*Where to find one:* Inquire at local restaurants or check the classified section of the newspaper to find a bartender.

*Cost:* The fee for this service can range from five dollars to ten dollars an hour with a 4-hour minimum. A gratuity of 15 percent can be given if you are especially pleased with the service rendered.

*Alternatives:* If the cost factor seems prohibitive, there is always the choice of calling on a good friend. Just be sure to pick someone who is familiar with bar service.

*When to have the bartender arrive:* Ask bartenders to arrive at least one hour before party time.

*Responsibilities:* It is the bartender's responsibility to set up the bar, cut the fruit, tend the bar, and at the end of the evening, to break down the bar.

*Operating the bar:* It is important for you to provide the bartender with the tools he or she will be needing:

> bar fruit—an assortment of lemons, limes, olives, oranges, and cherries.
> a cutting board and knife
> a corkscrew
> a cocktail stirrer (chopsticks work great!)
> cocktail napkins
> a bar rag or dishcloth
> a trash receptacle
> two pitchers—for water and juice
> ashtrays for the bar
> containers for ice
> backups for liquor, ice, soda
> (be sure to have bottle caps saved for keeping leftovers fresh!)

*Appropriate dress:* Black pants or skirt and a white shirt or blouse; black bow ties and black vest optional.

## Waitresses and Waiters

*Number needed:* For a buffet, it is good to figure one waiter or waitress per twenty people. For a sit-down dinner, one for every ten people would be needed.

*Where to find them:* Again, the best source to find these people is through your local restaurants or newspapers.

*Cost:* Price is five dollars to ten dollars an hour, generally with a four-hour minimum. Negotiate the wage according to their skills. Again, a 15 percent gratuity can be rendered. If you find a good service person, inquire with them as to people they are comfortable working with who may also be available.

*Staff arrival:* Ask all service people to arrive one to two hours before partytime. Sometimes it's a good idea to have one service person arrive two hours early to help with food preparation.

*Responsibilities:* Have your kitchen as neat and tidy as possible when the staff arrives so they will be aware of how it should look *after* the party! When they do arrive, it is up to you to assign them to what needs to be done. Last-minute food preparation or room setup can be left to reliable staff while you get yourself ready for the party. Once the party starts, each service person should be assigned separate responsibilities, such as taking coats, bringing out and passing food platters with cocktail napkins, refilling from the kitchen, and actually serving at the buffet table or guest table.

Throughout the party, ask all staff to maintain the party atmosphere as they clean discarded plates, cups, and napkins and empty ashtrays. At the end of dessert, service should be involved in cleanup, washing platters, rinsing rentals (if using), and disposing of trash.

It is important to inform staff on arrival of the type of party, who the guest of honor is, a detailed description of the menu being served, and type of time schedule on which you want the party to run.

*Dress:* Service people generally have their own standard attire. It usually consists of all black or black and white. Be sure to clarify with service ahead of time what they have available and what you desire.

NOTE: It's important to remember that these people are professionals. Treating them with the respect they deserve will make your (and their) party experience all the better. Remember, the staff is actually an extension of you yourself as the host or hostess all during the party, helping your guests to have the best evening possible!

## Rentals

If your party is large and you do not desire paper service, rentals of china and glassware is the answer. Be sure to call at least two weeks in advance. (Around Christmas, even earlier is a good idea.)

*Where to locate:* Check your Yellow Pages for listings under party rentals. If you cannot locate companies in your area, check with your local J.C.'s or Knights of Columbus organizations. They usually have large quantities of party supplies for their own affairs.

*Cost:* For a sit-down dinner, figure approximately five dollars to ten dollars for complete service. In addition, chairs, tables, coffee urns, ashtrays, linens, and so forth, are all available. Be sure to check prices in advance.

The best way to establish what you need is to run through the party in your mind from start to finish. Make your list *before* you call. Rental companies carry everything from tents to extra refrigerators, so you can generally count on them for all your party needs.

*Delivery:* Rentals will be delivered the day before the party, generally in wooden crates. They will be picked up usually the day after the party. You are responsible for rinsing and repacking the crates (have staff assist). (Be careful, because you will be charged for breakage!)

## Buffet Service

*Setting up:* Plates, utensils and napkins are put to one end of the buffet table and this, of course, is where the line will start. Take into consideration your room space when choosing which side the line will start from. Easy access away from the buffet table is very important, as your guests will be carrying full plates. After plates and utensils, we find it best to place rice or starch, then main course, then vegetable, salad, and bread.

*Service:* It is best to have your staff at the buffet table serving guests everything but salad and bread, letting guests help themselves to these. Have one service person be responsible for keeping the buffet table filled. Extra plates of food should be warming in the kitchen, ready to be placed out. After everyone has had a first helping, leave one person behind buffet table to serve second helpings and have the other go into the party to collect empty plates. Be sure to leave the buffet table intact until everyone has really had enough!

## Sit-Down Dinner Service

There are three types of service to choose from within the realm of the sit-down dinner:

1. Plate Service. Food is prepared in kitchen on each plate and brought out to the seated guest. The standard rule is to serve from the left, remove from the right.
2. French Service. Food is prepared and served on platters, which are passed by the staff, who actually serve each guest individually.
3. English Service. Food is prepared and served on platters, which are passed by the guests at each table.

In all cases, the place settings (including cups and saucers if the table is big enough) are laid out before guests arrive, and if you are serving a cold appetizer it's best to have that already on the table on top of the dinner plate. If you are using French or English service, the dinner plate would be left when the appetizer is cleared. For Plate service, staff would clear all plates, bringing the dinner plates into the kitchen.

At the end of the main course, ask staff to wait until all guests at a table have finished eating before beginning to clear. Dessert can be served as coffee and tea are being poured.

Chapter 15

# Tips from the Masters on Making Your Affair Beautiful!

## Garnishing and Decor

THE ATMOSPHERE in which your food is presented is every bit as important as the fare itself. Within the realm of the low budget, beautiful flowers, baskets, and soft lighting can work wonders. Designing the ambiance of your party is an especially interesting and creative part of the party preparation. Use your imagination, your personal sense of style, and set the scene for a terrific party to happen in.

### Ferns and Flowers for Buffet and Food Platter Garnish

*Ferns:* All types of ferns and greenery, such as lemon leaf, hair fern, leather leaf and palm leaves, are one of the best buys in making your affair beautiful. You might want to check out florist wholesalers in your city where ferns are sold in bunches at a very low cost. Three market-size bunches are plenty for buffet and platter garnish. A retail florist should also be able to supply you with ferns at a still very reasonable cost. Be sure to contact a retail florist early though, and let them know what you will be needing.

*Flowers:* Seasonal flowers are usually your best bet. If you have a garden, be sure to take advantage of it. When choosing flowers, pick colors that coordinate with your food and room decor. Remember that flowers are sold individually as well as by the bunch. Sometimes a few exotic flowers are more dramatic then bunches of the same kind.

*Food platter garnish:* As well as using ferns and flowers on your platters, try vegetable greens. Kale, chickory, and mustard greens are three excellent choices, since they are inexpensive and very durable. They can be spread under your hors d'oeuvres as well as around the sides, highlighted by a few destemmed blossoms for a classic effect.

### Flower Display

Oasis is the trick here. "Oasis" is a block of foam which holds both water and flowers. Available at your florist, it can be cut to any size you desire.

*To use oasis:* Soak foam in water. Meanwhile, make a container for oasis out of heavy-duty aluminum foil. Then place foam in foil and stick flower stems into foam. This will keep the flowers beautiful throughout the party. Used in this manner, a vase will not be needed. The foam in the foil can be placed directly on the table and covered with greenery.

### Baskets

Baskets are inexpensive and readily available. We recommend purchasing a variety of sizes as well as basket trays. Keep your eyes open for them at five-and-dime stores and flea markets. We feel you can never have too many. We use them for breads, hors d'oeuvres, crudités, utensils, and rolled napkins. They really dress up the buffet table.

### Linens

To cover an unattractive table to be used in the buffet, you can do wonders with several yards of fabric.

Simply stretch the fabric first over the top of the table and secure with staples. Then pleat fabric around the sides and front, working from one side to the other.

### Lighting

Soft, indirect lighting is generally preferable. Candlelight is often a good choice, because it is inexpensive and especially beautiful. White votive-size candles placed in clear glass votive holders and put on each table or grouped together on the buffet table can have a lovely effect at a very low cost.

## Crudités

Crudités hors d'oeuvres are so beautifully visual we have elected to include them in this chapter. They are ideal to have on the buffet table when guests arrive.

*Preparation:* There are many ways of preparing and presenting the vegetables for Crudités. The following is Russell Bennett's personal design.

1. Carrots. Best to use large, thick carrots. Wash well and cut into 3-inch pieces. Then slice lengthwise as thinly as possible. (A vegetable slicer such as a Miracle Slicer can be useful here.) Next, feather one end and place in cold water.
2. Broccoli and Cauliflower. Remove flowerets from stem. (Reserve rest of vegetable for use in soup.) Blanch flowerets by dropping into boiling water and then plunging into cold water. (Broccoli should be blanched in boiling water 1 minute; cauliflower for 3 minutes.) Blanching will deepen color and make vegetables more tender and digestable.
3. Green beans. Snap ends and blanch 5 minutes.
4. Red Pepper. Cut into ¾-inch thick circles.
5. Zucchini and Summer Squash. Zucchini—wash well and slice thinly on the diagonal. Summer squash—notch lengthwise in five places around squash, then slice thinly in circles.
6. Cucumber. Cut in the same manner as zucchini, above.
7. Spring Onion or Scallion. Trim both ends leaving about 1½ inch of green. Then slash bottom of white tip in star pattern, and fan out.
8. Cherry Tomatoes. Rinse and remove green stems.

### Cabbage Crock for Dip

1. Be sure to pick a cabbage whose outer leaves are intact. Red cabbage is usually a good choice.

2. Fan out as many leaves on outside as possible to create flowerlike effect.
3. Slice off bottom of cabbage so it will sit level.
4. Cut a circle in top of cabbage and peel out inside. A melon baller is a helpful tool for this. This will create a cavity that a small bowl can be fitted into and filled with dip.

### Arranging the Crudités

Using a circular tray if possible, place cored cabbage in middle of back rim.

1. Making circular rows starting with the outside, begin by arranging carrots along outside rim, feather top up.
2. Next row, arrange clumps of broccoli and cauliflower flowerets, alternating.
3. Next (third row), place zucchinis all around.
4. Fourth row, place yellow squash all around.
5. Fifth row, place cucumbers all around.
6. In hole left in center, place cherry tomatoes.
7. Stick green beans in clumps of broccoli and cauliflowers, standing them up.
8. Break red pepper circle and drape over broccoli clumps.

## Conclusion

The best tip we can give you on having a perfect affair is to have your party reflect you yourself as much as possible. A party is a celebration of life, and *your* party will always do best as a reflection and celebration of *your* life. Follow your instincts, take a few chances, and try always to have the confidence to know that it will all work out in the long run, just as it should. Once the effort has been put in and the time and care invested, an affair can hardly help be anything but beautiful. Enjoy!

Dear Friends,

The party's never *really* over. . . . We hope these recipes and ideas forever continue to fill your life with great affairs and, of course, no regrets. Thanks for participating in *our* affair!

With Best Wishes,

A. Annechild

R. Bennett

# Index